THE ESSENCE OF

COMPUTER GRAPHICS

THE ESSENCE OF COMPUTING SERIES

Selected published titles

The Essence of Artificial Intelligence
The Essence of Compilers
The Essence of Computing Projects – A Student's Guide
The Essence of Databases
The Essence of Data Structures using C++
The Essence of Discrete Mathematics
The Essence of Distributed Systems
The Essence of Expert Systems
The Essence of Human–Computer Interaction
The Essence of Java Programming
The Essence of Logic
The Essence of Program Design
The Essence of Programming Using C++
The Essence of Structures Systems Analysis Techniques
The Essence of Z

THE ESSENCE OF

COMPUTER GRAPHICS

Peter Cooley

Prentice Hall

An imprint of **Pearson Education**

Harlow, England · London · New York · Reading, Massachusetts · San Francisco
Toronto · Don Mills, Ontario · Sydney · Tokyo · Singapore · Hong Kong · Seoul
Taipei · Cape Town · Madrid · Mexico City · Amsterdam · Munich · Paris · Milan

Pearson Education Ltd
Edinburgh Gate
Harlow
Essex CM20 2JE
England

and Associated Companies around the World.

Visit us on the World Wide Web at:
www.pearsoneduc.com

First edition 2001

© Pearson Education Limited 2001

ISBN 0130-16283-3

British Library Cataloguing-in-Publication Data
A catalogue record for this book can be obtained from the British Library

Library of Congress Cataloging-in-Publication Data
Cooley, Peter.
  The essence of computer graphics / Peter Cooley.
    p. cm. — (The essence of computing)
  Includes bibliographical references and index.
  ISBN 0-13-016283-3
  1. Computer graphics. I. Title. II. Series.

  T385.C658   2000
  006.6—dc21   00-041656

10 9 8 7 6 5 4 3 2 1
05 04 03 02 01

Typeset in 10/12 pt Times by 35
Printed in Great Britain by Henry Ling Ltd.,
at the Dorset Press, Dorchester, Dorset.

Contents

Preface ix

1 Hardware and software *1*
  1.1 Hardware developments *1*
  1.2 Software developments *3*
  1.3 Summary *6*
  1.4 Further reading *6*
  1.5 Exercises *8*

2 Two-dimensional coordinate geometry *9*
  2.1 Introduction *9*
  2.2 Points *10*
  2.3 Cartesian and polar coordinates *12*
  2.4 Circular arcs *14*
  2.5 Lines *17*
  2.6 Homogeneous coordinates of a point *20*
  2.7 Parametric form of straight line *21*
  2.8 Summary *22*
  2.9 Further reading *23*
  2.10 Exercises *23*

3 Two-dimensional shapes *24*
  3.1 Introduction *24*
  3.2 Types of 2D shapes *26*
  3.3 Transformation of shapes *29*
  3.4 Summary *32*
  3.5 Further reading *33*
  3.6 Exercises *33*

4 Processing 2D shapes *34*
  4.1 Introduction *34*
  4.2 Inside/outside tests *34*
  4.3 Boolean operations on 2D shapes *38*
  4.4 Inflation and deflation *40*

4.5 Geometric properties *44*
4.6 Summary *46*
4.7 Further reading *47*
4.8 Exercises *47*

5 Curves *49*
5.1 Parametric cubic curves *49*
5.2 Bézier curves *51*
5.3 Space curves *55*
5.4 Summary *59*
5.5 Further reading *60*
5.6 Exercises *60*

6 Three dimensions *62*
6.1 Introduction *62*
6.2 Homogeneous coordinates *62*
6.3 Transformations *66*
6.4 Polygonal plane surfaces *69*
6.5 Intersecting planes *71*
6.6 Summary *72*
6.7 Further reading *73*
6.8 Exercises *73*

7 Modelling natural objects *75*
7.1 Introduction *75*
7.2 What is a fractal? *76*
7.3 A simple example *77*
7.4 Fractal classification *79*
7.5 Fractal construction *80*
7.6 Self-squaring fractals *83*
7.7 Summary *92*
7.8 Further reading *92*
7.9 Exercises *93*

8 Solid modelling *94*
8.1 Introduction *94*
8.2 Boundary representation (B-rep) *95*
8.3 Constructive solid geometry (CSG) *99*
8.4 Modulated cross-sections *102*
8.5 Octrees *105*
8.6 Summary *110*
8.7 Further reading *111*
8.8 Exercises *112*

9 The visible surface problem *114*

9.1 Introduction *114*
9.2 Painter's algorithm *118*
9.3 Warnock's algorithm *120*
9.4 Scan line algorithm *122*
9.5 Summary *126*
9.6 Further reading *127*
9.7 Exercises *127*

10 Pixel mapping *129*

10.1 Introduction *129*
10.2 Bresenham's line algorithm *129*
10.3 Bresenham's circle algorithm *133*
10.4 Filling algorithms *135*
10.5 Summary *139*
10.6 Further reading *139*
10.7 Exercises *140*

11 High realism *141*

11.1 Introduction *141*
11.2 True perspective *142*
11.3 Ray casting *143*
11.4 Ray tracing *144*
11.5 Polygon rendering techniques *150*
11.6 Texture *154*
11.7 Shadows and reflections *158*
11.8 Summary *159*
11.9 Further reading *161*
11.10 Exercises *161*

12 Some advanced techniques *163*

12.1 Introduction *163*
12.2 Morphing *164*
12.3 Animation *168*
12.4 Nesting *173*
12.5 Image enhancement *177*
12.6 Charting *183*
12.7 Summary *190*
12.8 Further reading *191*
12.9 Exercises *192*

Index 194

Preface

Welcome

The first time that I watched a graph being drawn by a digital computer linked to a pen plotter, I realised three things:

- the potential of Computer Graphics was immense
- the cost of the technology was also immense
- the programming and operational problems were formidable

The year was 1964, and the computer in question was an Elliot 803, in its own air-conditioned environment. It read in its program and data from 5-hole punched paper tape, and output the results either to tape or to plotter, hence my comment about programming and operational problems. At today's prices, the capital cost of the equipment was about £1M, not to mention the running costs, hence my comment about prohibitive cost. Younger readers will find these facts almost incredible. The intervening years have witnessed a reduction in cost and an improvement in ease of use that is truly amazing. That leaves my first conclusion: the immense potential. Welcome to the wonderful world of Computer Graphics. I still find it fascinating and stimulating, and I hope to be able to share my enthusiasm with you.

Applications

In the early years of Computer Graphics, most applications were scientific, funded by governments, universities, armed services, and international corporations. A sure sign that a new computer technology has come of age is when the hardware/software system 'pays for itself', by making possible the previously impossible, speeding up operations, significantly increasing productivity, or giving the organisation using it a competitive edge. One of the first applications to demonstrate this was computer aided drafting. By the 1970s, large corporations like Ford, Boeing, and General Motors could show drafting productivity improvements of 100% or more, and costs were recoverable in about three years.

It is generally the case that advances in graphics software come first, absorb much of the capacity of the contemporary hardware, and cannot be widely adopted until the cost of the hardware falls. Graphics displays of the random-scan type were horrendously expensive. The direct view storage tube greatly reduced the capital cost, and modern high-resolution raster displays have made good quality high-speed graphics available to all. Of course, much early software was for pure research, with no thought of recovering the cost of development. Another remarkable facet of the history of this technology is just how rapidly commercial software houses entered the market.

The current situation is that it is hard to find an area of human activity for which there are no Computer Graphics applications. Applications exist for:

- games, both arcade and intellectual (Chess, Bridge, etc),
- photography (still and video),
- animation,
- newspaper, Magazine and Television production,
- scientific research,
- computer aided Design and Manufacture,
- image enhancement,
- charting,
- electronic commerce....

What to put in?

This cornucopia of applications presented a major problem for the author. Obviously, there are certain fundamental concepts that must be included. Less obvious are algorithms that are implemented in hardware and are therefore totally transparent to the contemporary user. I decided that Bresenham's line and circle algorithms were not only of historical interest, but also reveal important 'tricks of the trade' that can be used to solve other problems.

Other decisions were much more difficult. For example, how many examples of solutions to the Visible Surface problem should be presented? The compromise here was to include landmark algorithms that could be readily presented in the available space, and that exemplify paradigms found in other applications. The Advanced Topics in the final chapter were selected because of the author's experience and of the need for this textbook to be thoroughly up to date.

Approach

The reader is not expected to have progressed in mathematics beyond a good GCSE. However, that level of knowledge is *vital*, and it would be a good idea to revise areas such as mensuration, Pythagoras's theorem, trigonometry, natural logarithms, coordinate geometry, matrices and differentiation, if you have forgotten what you did know. Beyond these essential topics, new mathematical material is introduced rather slowly and carefully, but experienced readers can skip if they wish.

The programming language chosen for all the examples is C++. C programmers need not be concerned at the change to the object-oriented language: the only difference they will notice is in the way that parameters are passed by functions. Admittedly, C++ is not the most readable of languages, but (like English) it is so widely used as to make it the obvious choice for a book of this nature and potential readership. If it is totally new to you, then help is available in the *Essence of Computing* series: *The Essence of Programming Using C++*, by Douglas Bell.

Many people (the author included) find it hard to visualise 3D objects when they are represented in 2D. My approach has been to present carefully chosen pictorial views of all the solid objects that are described or analysed in the text. I have also suggested on two occasions that it might be helpful to make a cardboard model of certain objects as an aid to visualisation and understanding the techniques that are described.

How did we all manage before Internet access became so widely available? There are so many excellent web sites for the student of Computer Graphics that selection was again a problem. I have provided the URLs of about half a dozen and they illustrate such diverse topics as 3D sections, morphing, and mechanism animation.

Any questions?

If you have questions or comments, I will be delighted to hear from you at my e-mail address:

peter.cooley@btinternet.com

Details of *The Essence of Computer Graphics* web site may be obtained by email request.

Peter Cooley
31 March 2000

Icon (p. 135) reprinted by permission from Microsoft Corporation.

CHAPTER 1

Hardware and software

1.1 **Hardware developments**

Most readers will be familiar with the cathode-ray tube (CRT) in its domestic guise as the display tube of a television set. When electrons strike the phosphor coating on the tube, light is emitted. The technology is much older than television and was first used by scientists and engineers in the form of the oscilloscope. In an oscilloscope, the deflection of the beam is proportional to a transient voltage, and the image on the screen indicates how this voltage varies with time.

In the 1950s, workers at the Massachusetts Institute of Technology (MIT) experimented with the use of a *computer* to control the deflection of the electron beam. Two pairs of deflection plates control the position of the beam. The elements of such a device are illustrated in Fig. 1.1.

By using digital-to-analogue converters, the output of the computer is changed to voltages across the x and y deflection plates. If the voltages steering the beam change at a constant rate, then the beam will trace a straight line,

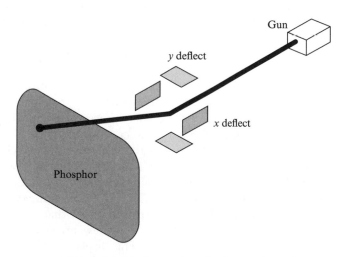

Figure 1.1 Random-scan cathode ray tube.

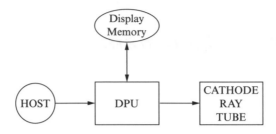

Figure 1.2 The architecture of a computer with a display processor.

visible to a viewer. This device is known as a **random-scan** or **calligraphic** CRT because the beam can be moved directly from any position to any other position. If the beam intensity is turned off, the beam can be moved to a new position without causing any visible display.

The 1960's were a time of significant advances in graphics hardware. The **direct-view storage tube** (DVST) became the standard low-cost output device. The DVST could retain an image indefinitely, thus relieving the computer of the necessity of continuously updating the display. This device was marketed by **Tektronix**, and packaged as a terminal that used special character sequences to invoke its graphics capabilities. The DVST is not a real-time device. Like a drawing on a 'magic slate', everything remains visible until it is all erased. The drawing can be added to at any time, but the kind of selective erasure exemplified by a 'cut and paste' operation is not possible.

The development of the **display processor** allowed the generation of interactive real-time graphics on the random-scan CRT. The display processor is a special-purpose computer with a limited set of instructions that it can execute very rapidly. Its primary task is to keep the CRT refreshed at a rate that makes the display appear smooth and flicker-free. Graphical entities that are defined on the host are placed in a special memory called the 'display memory' or 'display file', which is accessed by the display-processing unit (DPU), as in Fig. 1.2.

The host computer then needs to define graphical primitives only once. When these primitives have been sent on to the display processor, the host is free for other tasks. The functions of the display processor are incorporated in most present graphics systems, although advances in technology have allowed the functionality of the earliest systems to be reduced to one or two chips.

The next era of computer graphics (1970–80) was notable for the arrival of raster graphics. Reductions in the cost of solid-state memory made it feasible to construct systems that used a raster-scan CRT. In raster graphics, the image is stored as an array of picture elements, or pixels, rather than as a set of line segments, as it is with random-scan displays. The pixels are stored in a special memory area, known as the 'frame buffer'. The display hardware scans the frame buffer, usually at a rate of 50–70 scans per second, refreshing the display line by line, much in the way that television images are produced. Graphical output primitives, such a line segments, circles and text, are displayed by turning on or off pixels in the frame buffer that approximate the primitive. This process is known as 'scan conversion'. As a result of this new technology, many scan-conversion algorithms were developed. The personal computer and early workstations were developed during this period. In their architectures, the frame buffer is part of the memory of the computer and the graphics display is not a peripheral, but an integral part of the computer. New ways of interacting with the computer, such as through mouse-controlled menu-driven interfaces, were developed in the 1970s.

During the 1980s, the focus shifted somewhat. Powerful graphics workstations have become the standard tool of engineers, scientists, animators, graphic artists and architects. Such workstations not only place enormous computing power in the hands of the user, but also provide a powerful set of graphics tools, such as libraries of graphics routines and easy-to-use visual interfaces. Moreover, with networking the access to additional resources is almost unlimited. Workstations can produce images from simulations at speeds close to those previously associated with supercomputers.

The last decade of the twentieth century witnessed very high resolution graphics displays with practically unlimited colour selection. Most desktop computers now have a multi-media capability and the DVD (Digital Versatile Disk) format can store a full-length feature film. Still images are readily captured by computer by scanning or downloading from a digital camera. Moving images (with sound) are downloadable from video cameras or taken directly from a TV signal.

1.2 Software developments

The low cost of the direct-view storage tube allowed the development of basic graphics packages, such as PLOT10, that could be transported from system to system. Thus, the DVST spawned systems for computer drafting and computer-aided design that were affordable by medium-sized corporations. As a typical installation could increase productivity by a factor of two, such systems paid for themselves in 2–3 years. A new generation of draftsmen preferred to work in this way, and the change in attitude encouraged the development of software for computer-aided manufacturing, finite element analysis, simulation, etc.

The advent of the display processor made possible other facilities, such as user interaction with the displayed image. Sutherland's *Sketchpad* project demonstrated the potential of such a system, and researchers began a thorough examination of the issues involved. The importance of data structures for graphics was recognised, algorithms were developed and the paradigms that characterise modern computer graphics were formulated.

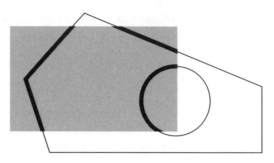

Figure 1.3 Clipping

The widespread use of computer graphics sparked considerable interest in the development of a standard graphics programming language. A European group was formed which produced the Graphics Kernel System (GKS). The International Standards Organisation adopted GKS in 1984, and formal adoption of GKS by the American National Standards Institute (ANSI) followed soon afterwards.

Amongst the important concepts considered in GKS was the **viewport**. The early graphics displays were exactly that: graphics (and nothing but graphics) filling the entire screen. Most modern operating systems provide for user-defined rectangles in which the graphic entities are to be displayed. It is important to distinguish between a **window** and a **viewport**. Typically, a window is the property of an application, and everything that the application displays is in one or more of its windows. An application can have many windows at its disposal. A viewport is a part of a window in which graphics may be displayed. The graphics viewport can be almost the entire window, but never all of it because all windows systems have a caption bar at the top and various controls around the sides that reduce the area available for the graphics.

Hence, there are three computations to be done whenever a graphics entity is to be displayed in a viewport:

- the scale at which it should be drawn
- the position at which it should be drawn
- how much of it is actually visible in the viewport.

The first two questions are addressed in Chapter 2. The third problem is illustrated in Fig. 1.3.

The grey shaded rectangle represents the viewport. Clearly, the bottom and the right-hand edges of the pentagon cannot be seen through the viewport. There are two edges to the left of the pentagon that are clipped once each by horizontal edges of the viewport. One edge is clipped twice, and the circle is clipped twice. In refreshed displays, this clipping is done by routines built into the display processor, as there is insufficient time for software-based computations.

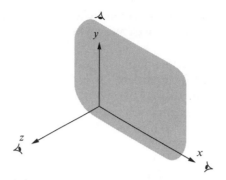

Figure 1.4 Positive z axis is out of screen, towards viewer.

The arrival of raster graphics demanded software that could rapidly render certain primitive elements on the screen. A moderately complex diagram can typically have around 100 lines, and also a significant number of circles. Those lines and circles have to be refreshed at up to 70 times per second, and so rendering speed is vital. All arithmetic must be integer arithmetic, as the necessary speed is impossible with floating-point arithmetic. It turned out that at least one vital algorithm (for straight lines) had already been written for driving an incremental plotter. Bresenham's line algorithm was incorporated into the display processor along with other fast routines for rendering circles, rectangles, ellipses, etc.

It was realised in the early days of computer graphics that 3-dimensional objects could be represented on a computer screen. The object can be made to appear 3-dimensional if it can be rotated in real time. Failing that, computations can be done of the object as seen from various positions and the results stored for frame-by-frame display. It is essential to have some convention as to what is a positive rotation of the object. Figure 1.4 shows one such convention: an anticlockwise rotation as seen from one of the three 'eye-balls' is taken as positive.

Figure 1.4 is known as a *right-handed* coordinate system. Right-handed systems are conventional in mathematics, physics and engineering. The effect of this convention (to be used throughout this book) is that the larger the z coordinate of a vertex, the nearer it is to the viewer. A positive (anti-clockwise) rotation around the z axis will appear as anti-clockwise to the viewer.

Researchers in computer graphics were faced with the problem of how to model solid objects within the computer system. The 'wire-frame' technique is not satisfactory as it is difficult to detect the orientation of a particular surface. Moreover, there are many possibilities for ambiguity. The two practical modelling techniques discussed in Chapter 8 were developed. Ian Braid's landmark publication 'Designing with Volumes' showed that a practicable scheme was to combine primitive, easily defined solids together using Boolean operators.

Many years were to elapse before commercial packages were available, but at least the fundamental problem presented by a geometric model could now be addressed.

The so-called 'visible surface problem' can be expressed like this. Given a complex opaque object, which parts of its surface are visible to the viewer and should be rendered in the display? Workers soon concluded that some form of 'divide and conquer' paradigm was required. The difficulty was in choosing one that would work, given the high cost of memory and the low speed of contemporary processors. Chapter 9 is devoted entirely to an examination of this topic.

The advent of high-resolution raster graphics has placed new demands on the ingenuity of programmers. Applications such as flight simulators require the generation of highly realistic images in real time. Newspapers, television and cinema all make extensive use of computer graphics. It is now possible to create convincing simulations of just about any event, from walking around inside a planned building, to a missile attack, to cosmic events such as the beginning and the end of the universe. Many of the images produced by such software are of photographic quality. That is to say, only an expert could tell the difference between a photograph of a real scene and a computer rendering from a geometric model of that scene. Chapter 11 treats some of the techniques that have been evolved.

1.3 Summary

- The hardware of computer graphics has progressed from *random-scan CRT* via the *direct-view storage tube* to high-resolution colour raster graphics in less than forty years.
- The display-processing unit relieved the host computer of the task of refreshing the graphics display and made computer graphics far quicker and cheaper.
- The modern graphical user interface owes much to Sutherland's *Sketchpad* software.
- The Graphics Kernel System (GKS) is the established international standard.
- Computer graphics applications are now widely used throughout science, industry, education, entertainment and communications.

1.4 Further reading

As this chapter has sought to show, there is a vital interaction between the hardware and the software of computer graphics. The following books and papers are recommended either as an introduction to the subject or because of a specific reference above.

Amantides, J., 'Realism in Computer Graphics: A Survey', *IEEE Computer Graphics and Applications*, Vol. 1, No. 1, pp. 44–56, 1987. A comprehensive review of the then state of the art. It is not altogether surprising that progress since then has been incremental.

Braid, I. C., *Designing with Volumes (Second Edition)*, Cantab Press, 1974. Based upon Braid's Cambridge University thesis, this work demonstrated conclusively that Constructive Solid Geometry was practicable for 3D design.

Bresenham, J. E., 'Algorithm for Computer Control of a Digital Plotter', *IBM Systems Journal*, Vol. 4, No.1, pp. 25–30, 1965. An ironically titled paper, as the application of the algorithm is now universally in raster graphics.

Bresenham, J. E., 'A Linear Algorithm for Incremental Digital Display of Circular Arcs', *Comm. Of ACM*, Vol. 20, No. 2, pp. 100–106, 1977. A very significant paper, which showed how curved graphics elements could be rendered using only integer arithmetic. Notice how the hardware has changed in the twelve years since his IBM publication.

Cooley, P., 'Mechanical drafting on a desktop computer', *Computer-aided design*, Vol. 11, No. 2, pp. 79–84, 1979. One of the first low-cost, single-user systems.

Graphical Kernel System, ISO 7492, International Standards Organisation, 1985. The actual standard specification. Not an easy read.

Graphical Kernel System for Three Dimensions, ISO 8805, International Standards Organisation, 1986. The 3D extension to the 1985 standard.

Hearn, D. and M. P. Baker, *Computer Graphics C Version (Second Edition)*, Prentice Hall Inc., 1997. A well-illustrated (and therefore somewhat expensive) textbook, which has stood the test of time while it has continually improved. There is also a version with examples in Pascal.

Hopgood, F. R. A., D. A. Duce, J. A. Gallop, and D. C. Sutcliffe, *Introduction to the Graphical Kernel System: GKS*, Academic Press, London, 1983. A worthy attempt at making GKS comprehensible to mere mortals.

Lathrop, O., *The Way Computer Graphics Work*, John Wiley and Sons Ltd, 1997. Theory of computer graphics for the non-computer scientist.

Masson, T., *CG101 (A Computer Graphics Industry Reference)*, New Riders, 1999. An industry survey and reference for the computer graphics newcomer. Facts, techniques, history, disciplines and key people are covered.

Plastock, R. A. and G. S. Kalley, *Shaum's Outline of Computer Graphics*, McGraw-Hill, New York, 1986. Chapter 12 is an introduction to GKS.

Sproull, R. F. and I. E. Sutherland, 'A Clipping Divider', *1968 Fall Joint Computer Conference*, pp. 765–775, Thompson Books, Washington, 1968. It was this paper that showed the way to speedy, low-cost solutions to the clipping problem.

Sutherland, I. E., '*SKETCHPAD*: A Man-Machine Graphical Communication System', *AFIPS Spring Joint Computer Conference*, pp. 329–346, Spartan Books, Baltimore, 1963. Truly a watershed in the history of computer graphics. What is now termed the *Graphical User Interface* (GUI) originates from this work.

Sutherland, I. E., R. F. Sproull, and R. A. Schumaker, 'A Characterisation of Ten Hidden-Surface Algorithms', *Computer Surveys*, Vol. 6, No. 1, pp. 1–55, 1974. A remarkable, scholarly review of a very difficult subject. This was the first serious attempt at classifying the various algorithms that had been developed at that time.

Vince, J., *The Language of Computer Graphics*, Phaidon Press Ltd., 1990. A dictionary of terms and concepts.

Exercises

1. Where was the first research done into using a computer to send signals to a cathode-ray tube?
2. List the major operational differences between the *random-scan CRT* and the *direct-view storage tube*.
3. How does a DPU speed up a refreshed display?
4. Of the *random-scan CRT*, the *direct-view storage tube* and *raster graphics*, which type of display has the greatest, and which has the least problem with 'flicker'?
5. When did the first mouse-controlled menu-driven interfaces appear?
6. How was it that Computer Drafting systems using DVST technology were able to 'pay for themselves'?
7. What is GKS and when was it adopted by the International Standards Organisation?
8. What is a viewport, and what is meant by 'clipping' in relation to a viewport?
9. What is a pixel?
10. What was the original application for Bresenham's line algorithm?
11. If the positive x axis is to the right, and the positive y axis is upwards, in which direction does the positive z axis point?

Two-dimensional coordinate geometry

2.1 **Introduction**

The earliest applications of computer graphics were for drawing simple diagrams, charts, and plans. A flow chart like that shown in Fig. 2.1 exemplifies
what the graphics hardware/software system must be capable of doing. Clearly,
the various features are generated by connecting points together in some way.
In Fig. 2.1, they are connected with either a straight line or a circular arc.

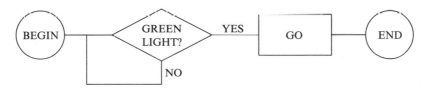

Figure 2.1 A simple diagram from lines and circular arcs.

You might ask: 'what about the text?' A simple, unadorned font can be
designed using only straight lines and circular arcs, like the rest of the diagram.
In order to display (or render) the above chart on a computer screen there are
five questions that have to be answered.

- In what part of the screen will the graphics have to fit? In other words:
  what is the size and position of the **viewport**?
- What are the overall dimensions of the graphics that are to be displayed?
- How should the graphics be scaled and positioned in the viewport?
- How are the component parts positioned relative to one another?
- What is the geometry of each component?

The component parts are positioned relative to one another by using coordinate geometry: specifically, cartesian coordinates (x, y). The geometry of each
component can be specified using a topology array that indicates how certain
cardinal points are to be connected. Once these data are available, it is possible
to compute the overall dimensions of the graphics display. Using these dimensions and the dimensions of the viewport, it is possible to map the display into

the area available. The aspect ratio of the viewport and the bounding rectangle of the graphics rarely coincide, so the top and bottom margins will generally be different in size from the left and right margins. Clearly, the positioning of a point in 2D and its relationship to the graphics display system is fundamental to any computer graphics application. So too are the drawing of lines and arcs, finding where two lines intersect, and determining if a point lies on a specific line. Hence, we will now examine these problems in some detail.

2.2 **Points**

In cartesian coordinates, a point in 2-dimensional space is specified by its distance from some vertical axis (usual symbol x) and its distance from some horizontal axis (usual symbol y). These parameters can be (and often are) floating-point numbers, rather than integers. Hence, a point P that is horizontally 3.5 units from the y axis and -1.7 vertically from the x axis may be described as a vector $\mathbf{P}$ using an equation such as:

$$\mathbf{P} = (3.5, -1.7)$$

What this equation implies is that, in order to get to point P (starting from the origin) it is necessary to move 3.5 units to the right and 1.7 units downwards (or -1.7 units upwards).

Points or pixels on a computer screen are *not* described in the same way. For the moment, we will suppose that the entire screen area is a graphics display, as illustrated in Fig. 2.2.

There are U pixel positions horizontally and they have addresses $0..U-1$. There are V pixel positions vertically and they have addresses $0..V-1$. Notice that both the horizontal and the vertical pixel positions are described like the columns and rows of an array, because that is exactly how they are stored within the computer system. Hence, the greater the value of the vertical pixel address the nearer it is to the *bottom* of the screen. This of course is the direct opposite of the convention for cartesian coordinates: the larger the y value the nearer it will be to the *top* of the screen.

Figure 2.2 Screen pixel addresses.

The other complicating factor when displaying points on a screen is the fact that pixel addresses are *integers*, whereas cartesian coordinates can be real (floating point) numbers. Hence, in order to display a shape on a computer screen the following steps are required:

1. Find the boundary values of the shape.
2. Compute a suitable scale and offset to fit the shape onto part of the screen.
3. Convert each pair of cartesian coordinates to a pixel address.
4. Set each pixel (and connect them with lines if necessary).

Example 2.1

The triangle shown below is to be displayed on a computer screen that has 1024 pixel columns and 768 pixel rows. What pixel addresses should points **P**, **Q**, and **R** have if the triangle is to appear centrally on the screen and occupy approximately half of the available width?

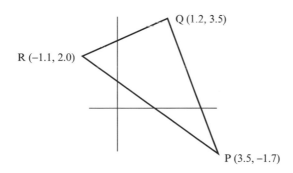

By inspection, we note:

Minimum value of x, $Xmin = -1.1$
Maximum value of x, $Xmax = 3.5$
Minimum value of y, $Ymin = -1.7$
Maximum value of y, $Ymax = 3.5$
Mean value of y, $Ymean = (Ymin + Ymax)/2 = (-1.7 + 3.5)/2 = 0.9$

The question states that approximately half the width of the screen is to be used, and that *Xmean* is to be at the centre of the screen. In other words, the pixel address of *Xmin* is to be 25% of 1024 = 256 and the pixel address of *Xmax* is to be 75% of 1024 = 768. There is a linear relationship between pixel column number, *I*, and coordinate units of the form

$$I = Ax + B$$

When $x = Xmin$, $I = 256$, and therefore $256 = -1.1A + B$
When $x = Xmax$, $I = 768$, and therefore $768 = 3.5A + B$

Solving these two equations simultaneously, we get

$512 = 4.6A$ and therefore $A = 111.3$, $B = 378.4$ and so $\boxed{I = 111.3x + 378.4}$

The coefficient A is a **scaling factor**; it measures the number of pixel positions that are used for each unit of x. To avoid distorting the shape, it is necessary to have the same scaling factor in the horizontal and vertical directions, and so we can use the value 111.3 pixels per unit in a similar equation relating J to y. As pixel rows are counted from the *top* of the screen, the sign of the scaling factor needs to be changed and so the equation is:

$J = -111.3y + C$

When $y = Ymean$, $J = 384$, and therefore $384 = -111.3 \times 0.9 + C$

Hence $C = 484.2$, and so $\boxed{J = -111.3y + 484.2}$

2.3 Cartesian and polar coordinates

In computer graphics applications it is often the case that, whereas the position of a point is stored in cartesian coordinates, useful computations require a radius and angular position. In theory, the conversion to polar coordinates is very straightforward. In practice, complications arise from the manner in which inverse trigonometric functions are computed, so it is necessary to examine how to compute an angular position accurately.

Look at Fig. 2.3, triangle OQP

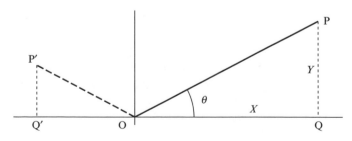

Figure 2.3 Cartesian and polar coordinates.

Clearly, $\tan\theta = Y/X$. Hence $\theta = \tan^{-1}(Y/X)$, and such an angle may be computed using the function `atan` available in the C++ <math.h> library. Unfortunately, the argument input to this function has first to be computed by dividing X into Y. There are two problems about this.

1. If X is zero (or very close to it) then we must avoid division by zero and return the value of θ as $\pm \pi/2$ radians.
2. If $X < 0$ then we can only get the correct angle (e.g. for triangle OQ'P') by adding π radians to $\tan^{-1}(Y/X)$.

In C++, a suitable function would look like this:

```
#include <math.h>

void CartToPolar (float x, float y, float & Radius, float & Angle)
{
const float pi = 4.0 * atan(1.0);

Radius = sqrt(x * x + y * y);
if (abs(x) < 0.0001)
    Angle = 0.5 * pi * abs(y) / y;
else
    {
    Angle = atan(y / x);
    if (y < 0.0)
        Angle = Angle + pi;
    }
}
```

Notice that (for clarity) `pi` is computed above using the function `atan`, whereas the value of π is generally available as a global constant. There is a function `atan2` in most C libraries that deals with problems 1 and 2 above.

The fact that all computers use radians as the unit of angular measurement, and yet humans think in degrees, is less of a problem than might at first appear. It is rare to encounter an application where the user is prompted to input an angle. Angles are generally computed from cartesian coordinates. Any necessary processing is done within the machine, and the results are displayed or plotted by converting back to cartesian within the machine. For completeness, a function for converting polar to cartesian is given below.

```
#include <math.h>

void PolarToCart (float Radius, float Angle, float & x, float & y)
{
x = Radius * cos(Angle);
y = Radius * sin(Angle);
}
```

2.4 **Circular arcs**

Most computer graphics display hardware has built-in routines for the display of complete circles. The algorithm used is by Bresenham, and it is described in detail in Chapter 10. It uses integer arithmetic for the rapid display of a full circle. However, there are many applications where a circular *arc* is required that begins or ends at a position other than some multiple of 45°. Figure 2.4 shows the outline of a simple cam that rotates about point O.

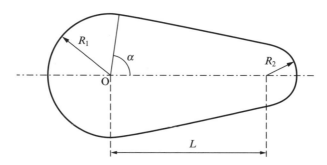

Figure 2.4 Cam with circular arcs.

Notice that the cam is fully and unambiguously defined by the dimensions R_1, R_2 and L, and that by the usual technical drawing convention, tangency is to be assumed in the absence of contradictory information. In order either to manufacture or to make an accurate drawing of this cam, there are several essential computations. We will concentrate on drawing the larger circular arc and hence we need the angle α, which is related to R_1, R_2 and L as follows:

$$\cos\alpha = (R_1 - R_2)/L$$

The only practicable way to compute an angle is to use a robust cartesian to polar function, like that detailed above. Such a function computes the angle from its tangent, so it will be necessary to input the opposite and adjacent sides of the relevant triangle. The correct triangle for computing angle α is shown in Fig. 2.5.

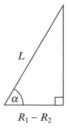

Figure 2.5 Trigonometry for Fig. 2.4.

In general, it will be possible to convert whatever trigonometric ratio is known to the tangent value. In the present example, Pythagoras's theorem gives the result:

$$\tan\alpha = \sqrt{[L^2 - (R_1 - R_2)^2]}/(R_1 - R_2)$$

Hence, drawing of the arc could commence at angle α and finish at $-\alpha$. However, the finish angle must be greater than the start angle, and so arc construction finishes at $2\pi - \alpha$. This provides another general rule about arc drawing: if the computed finish angle is less than or equal to the start angle then add 2π radians to the finish angle.

The actual display (rendering) of the arc is done by generating a suitable number of short straight lines, which are actually chords of an arc that starts at angle θ_1 and finishes at angle θ_2. Provided the length of the chord is well matched to the display, the human eye perceives these discreet straight lines as a continuous arc.

The selection of a suitable angular increment, $d\theta$, is complicated by the fact that the arc must end at precisely the right point after a whole number of steps from the start point. A length of about 8 pixels is usually suitable for the straight line. Hence

$$R\, d\theta \cong 8$$

$d\theta$ is then adjusted so that $(\theta_2 - \theta_1)/d\theta$ is an integer.

It is easy to write a function that will render such an arc, but it is likely to be very slow and inefficient if sines and cosines are computed at each increment of the angle. The following C++ code is typical of such an algorithm.

```cpp
#include <math.h>

void RenderArcSlow (float xc, float yc, float Radius, float
AngleStart, float AngleFinish, float Increment)

{
   float Theta = AngleStart;
   float Xstart, Ystart, Xfinish, Yfinish;

   Xstart = xc + Radius * cos(Theta);
   Ystart = yc + Radius * sin(Theta);
   Theta = AngleStart;

   while (Theta <= AngleFinish)
     {
     Theta = Theta + Increment;
```

```
    Xfinish = xc + Radius * cos(Theta);
    Yfinish = yc + Radius * sin(Theta);
    /* Draw a line from (Xstart, Ystart) to (Xfinish, Yfinish) */
    Xstart = Xfinish;
    Ystart = Yfinish;


  }

}
```

N.B. The comment:

```
/* Draw a line from (Xstart, Ystart) to (Xfinish, Yfinish) */
```

should be replaced by a call to a line drawing function of the C++ compiler used.

The reason why the function works slowly is that two transcendental functions (sine and cosine) have to be computed at each step within the loop. By making use of the compound angle formulae (detailed below), it is possible to eliminate these functions, which speeds things up considerably.

$$\cos(\theta + d\theta) = \cos\theta\cos d\theta - \sin\theta\sin d\theta$$

$$\sin(\theta + d\theta) = \sin\theta\cos d\theta + \cos\theta\sin d\theta$$

The cosine and sine of both the starting angle and the incremental angle are computed outside the loop. Inside the loop, we use the compound angle formulae to update the cosine of the current angle and store it in variable Temp. We then update the sine of the current angle and set the cosine equal to Temp. Hence, we compute the finish point of the current chord.

```
#include <math.h>

void RenderArcFast (float xc, float yc, float Radius,
          float AngleStart, float AngleFinish, float Increment)
{
  float Theta = AngleStart;
  float Xstart, Ystart, Xfinish, Yfinish, CosTheta, SinTheta,
       CosIncrement, SinIncrement, Temp;

  Theta = AngleStart;
  CosTheta = cos(Theta);
  SinTheta = sin(Theta);
  CosIncrement = cos(Increment);
  SinIncrement = sin(Increment);
  Xstart = xc + Radius * CosTheta;
  Ystart = yc + Radius * SinTheta;
  while (Theta <= AngleFinish)
```

```
    {
    Theta = Theta + Increment;
    Temp = CosTheta * CosIncrement - SinTheta * SinIncrement;
    SinTheta = CosTheta * SinIncrement + SinTheta * CosIncrement;
    CosTheta = Temp;
    Xfinish = xc + Radius * CosTheta;
    Yfinish = yc + Radius * SinTheta;
    /* Draw a line from (Xstart, Ystart) to (Xfinish, Yfinish) */
    Xstart = Xfinish;
    Ystart = Yfinish;
    }
}
```

N.B. The comment:

```
/* Draw a line from (Xstart, Ystart) to (Xfinish, Yfinish) */
```

should be replaced by a call to a line drawing function of the C++ compiler used.

2.5 **Lines**

In classical coordinate geometry, an infinite line is defined in terms of its gradient (m) and the value of y when $x = 0$ (k). These parameters are shown in Fig. 2.6, and the equation may be written as $y = mx + k$.

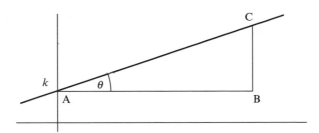

Figure 2.6 Straight line with gradient m and intercept k.

To see how this equation is established, look at triangle ABC, and let point C have cartesian coordinates (X, Y):

BC/AB $= \tan \theta = m$.

But AB $= X$ and BC $= Y - k$, hence $m = (Y - k)/X$
  Multiply both sides of the equation by X and then add k to both sides and we have

$$Y = mX + k$$

The above equation is what mathematicians call an 'explicit' equation. Given a particular value of x, the corresponding value of y can be calculated. The 'implicit' form is an equation with zero on the right hand side:

$$mX - Y + k = 0$$

It expresses what must be true for any point (X, Y) lying on the line. It is a linear equation (in the mathematical sense) and has the general form

$$ax + by + c = 0 \quad \text{which should be compared with} \quad mX - y + k = 0$$

in order to see that

$a = m$ (*the gradient of the line*)
$b = -1$
$c = k$ (*the intercept on the y axis*)

In two dimensions, *homogeneous coordinates* can be used to describe an infinite straight line as a **column vector** that looks like this.

$$\lambda = \begin{bmatrix} a \\ b \\ c \end{bmatrix} = \begin{bmatrix} m \\ -1 \\ k \end{bmatrix}$$

Provided the constant is *not* zero, it is permissible to multiply all the elements of the column vector by a constant in order to make the second element equal to −1, and hence compute the gradient and the intercept.

Example 2.2

What are the gradient and the intercept of this line?

$$\lambda = \begin{bmatrix} -2.5 \\ 2.5 \\ 5.0 \end{bmatrix}$$

To make the second element equal to −1, multiply all the elements by −1/2.5 to give

$$\lambda = \begin{bmatrix} 1.0 \\ -1.0 \\ -2.0 \end{bmatrix}$$

Hence, the gradient of the line is 1.0 and it intersects the y axis at -2.

When we multiply the column vector by $-1/2.5$, we are merely using the fact that the equation of the line is

$$-2.5x + 2.5y + 5.0 = 0$$

and it does not matter what we multiply zero by; the result will always be zero, hence

$$1.0x - 1.0y - 2.0 = 0$$

is exactly the same equation.

We will now find the homogeneous coordinates of any *finite* line between specific end points. The line starts at (X_1, Y_1) and ends at (X_2, Y_2), as shown in Fig. 2.7.

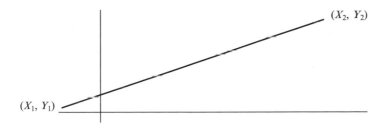

Figure 2.7 Finite line with end points specified.

The gradient of such a line is easily computed:

$$m = (Y_2 - Y_1)/(X_2 - X_1)$$

In classical coordinate geometry this line is

$$y - Y_1 = m(x - X_1)$$

Substituting for m and tidying up the equation to get zero on the right hand side gives

$$(Y_2 - Y_1)x + (X_1 - X_2)y + X_2 Y_1 - Y_2 X_1 = 0$$

from which we can immediately write the column vector

$$\lambda = \begin{bmatrix} Y_2 - Y_1 \\ X_1 - X_2 \\ X_2 Y_1 - Y_2 X_1 \end{bmatrix}$$

Example 2.3

Look at the infinite line in Example 2.2. As it intersects the y axis at -2, it passes through $(0, -2)$. With a gradient of 1.0, clearly it passes through $(2, 0)$. If we make these the end points of a finite line then

$$X_1 = 0; \ Y_1 = -2; \ X_2 = 2; \ Y_2 = 0$$

Substituting these values in the column vector

$$\lambda = \begin{bmatrix} Y_2 - Y_1 \\ X_1 - X_2 \\ X_2 Y_1 - Y_2 X_1 \end{bmatrix}$$

we get

$$\lambda = \begin{bmatrix} 0 + 2 \\ 0 - 2 \\ -4 - 0 \end{bmatrix} = \begin{bmatrix} 2 \\ -2 \\ -4 \end{bmatrix} = \begin{bmatrix} -0.5 \\ 0.5 \\ 1.0 \end{bmatrix}$$

which agrees with Example 2.2.

2.6 Homogeneous coordinates of a point

A point **P** (in 2D) is represented by the 3-element **row vector**

$$[u \quad v \quad w]$$

This maps to cartesian coordinates (x, y) as

$$x = u/w \quad \text{and} \quad y = v/w.$$

As with a column vector, all elements in a row vector may be multiplied by a non-zero constant. Hence

$$[u \quad v \quad w] = [u/w \quad v/w \quad 1] = [x \quad y \quad 1].$$

The scalar product of

$$[u \quad v \quad w] \begin{bmatrix} a \\ b \\ c \end{bmatrix} = ua + vb + wc$$

and it is axiomatic that if the point $[u \ v \ w]$ lies on the line $\begin{bmatrix} a \\ b \\ c \end{bmatrix}$ then the scalar product of row and column vectors is zero.

In computer graphics, we often need to know the perpendicular distance from a point to a line, and if the scalar product of the homogeneous coordinates of the point and the line is *not* zero, then we have a parameter that is directly proportional to this perpendicular distance. Suppose that the value of the parameter is q, then it may be shown that the perpendicular distance is

$$\frac{q}{\sqrt{a^2 + b^2}}$$

Notice the square root, which is generally bad news as it is computationally expensive to determine.

Two lines $\begin{bmatrix} a_1 \\ b_1 \\ c_1 \end{bmatrix}$ and $\begin{bmatrix} a_2 \\ a_2 \\ c_2 \end{bmatrix}$

will cross at (X, Y) provided they are not parallel. Hence X and Y are found by solving simultaneously

$$a_1 X + b_1 Y + c_1 = 0$$

and

$$a_2 X + b_2 Y + c_2 = 0$$

The homogeneous coordinates of the intersection point are

$$[b_1 c_2 - b_2 c_1 \quad a_2 c_1 - a_1 c_2 \quad a_1 b_2 - a_2 b_1]$$

If $a_1 b_2 - a_2 b_1 = 0$ then the lines are parallel, and it is pointless to compute the first and second elements of the row vector.

2.7 Parametric form of straight line

Computer graphics applications invariably deal with *finite* lines, whereas the above equation will find the intersection of two infinite, non-parallel lines. It is vital to have a simple way of testing if a computed point lies between the end points of *both* lines, and this is readily done by defining a parameter t that varies between 0 at the start point (X_0, Y_0) of a finite line and 1 at its finish point (X_1, Y_1). In other words, t is the fractional distance moved from the start of the line. We need two equations

$$x = X_0(1 - t) + X_1 t$$
$$y = Y_0(1 - t) + Y_1 t$$

which are subject to these boundary conditions:

$$0 \le t \le 1$$

From the above equations, when $t = 0$:

$$x = X_0 \quad \text{and} \quad y = Y_0$$

Similarly, when $t = 1$:

$$x = X_1 \quad \text{and} \quad y = Y_1$$

If we wish to know if a particular point is on a finite line, then we compute t using either

$$t = (x - X_0)/(X_1 - X_0)$$

or, if $X_0 = X_1$ (*vertical line*),

$$t = (y - Y_0)/(Y_1 - Y_0).$$

Notice that if $X_0 = X_1$ *and* $Y_0 = Y_1$ the line has degenerated to a point and can probably be ignored.

2.8 Summary

- The position of a point in 2D is normally specified by a pair of real numbers (x, y). The process of mapping such a point onto a graphics viewport has been investigated.
- The vital relationships between cartesian and polar coordinates have been examined in depth.
- Some solutions to the problem of drawing a circular arc (as opposed to a complete circle) have been presented.
- Homogeneous coordinates are an exceptionally useful tool for the graphics programmer. A line is represented by a 3-element column vector, and a point by a 3-element row vector. Fundamental relationships between points and lines have been given.

- Because we are always dealing with *finite* objects, it is vital to make use of the parametric form of a straight line when programming graphics procedures.

2.9 **Further reading**

The following books are recommended either to brush up your geometry, or for an in-depth look at some algorithms.

Bowyer, A. and J. R. Woodwark, *A Programmer's Geometry*, Butterworths, London, 1983. Lots of useful geometric results that can be readily converted to practicable algorithms.

Gasson, P. C., *Geometry of Spatial Forms*, Ellis Horwood, Chichester, 1983. Lots of useful geometry. Very good on homogeneous coordinates in both 2D and 3D.

Egerton, P. A. and W. S. Hall, *Computer Graphics: Mathematical First Steps*, Prentice Hall Europe, 1997. More elementary than Gasson, but none the worse for that.

Walker, B. S., J. R. Gurd and E. A. Drawneek, *Interactive Computer Graphics*, Edward Arnold, London, 1976. Very good on the topics of clipping and fast circular arc rendering.

Exercises

1. Find the pixel addresses of the vertices of the triangle specified in Example 2.1.
2. Plot on paper the following points. Determine the polar coordinates using a pocket calculator, and check that the function listed on page 13 gives the same results.

X	Y	radius	angle (radians)	angle (degrees)
1	1	1.41	0.7854	45
−1	−1	1.41	3.927	225
0	2	2.00	1.5708	90
0	−2	2.00	−1.5708	−90

3. In Example 2.2, what is the value of x when $y = 0$?
4. Sketch a graph for the line specified in Example 2.3. Does point (3, 1) lie on the infinite line?
5. Does a line from (3, 0) to (0, 3) cross a line from (0, 0) to (2, 4), and if so where?
6. Where does the line from (−1, 1) to (1, −1) cross a line from (0, −4) to (2, 0)? Does the intersection lie on *both* finite lines?

CHAPTER 3
Two dimensional shapes

3.1 **Introduction**

The flow chart shown in Fig. 2.1 is but one example of what could be drawn using a computer graphics system. The proper study of diagrams, charts, plans, etc. is called 'graph theory', and a few definitions in this section will help to illuminate what follows. Figure 3.1a depicts part of a road map. Figure 3.1b is a sectional view from an engineering drawing. Both the road map and the sectional view can be represented diagramatically by means of points and lines as in Fig. 3.2.

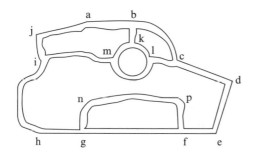

Figure 3.1a Road map.

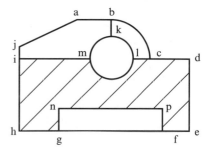

Figure 3.1b Engineering drawing.

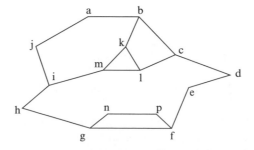

Figure 3.2 Graph equivalent to both Figures 3.1a and 3.1b.

The points a b c d e f g h i j k l m n p are referred to as 'nodes' and the connections between them are dubbed 'edges'. (Graph theorists usually refer to the connections as 'arcs', but 'edge' is the term adopted for this book, for obvious reasons.) The whole diagram is a 'graph'. The 'degree' of a node is the number of edges that have that node as an end-point. A node of degree two is referred to as a 2-node. Nodes a d e h g n p are 2-nodes. Nodes b c f g i k l m are 3-nodes.

A 'simple graph' is one in which there is never more than one edge joining a given pair of nodes. If there are two or more edges joining a pair of nodes then they are called 'multiple edges'. A 'loop' is an edge that has both end-points at the same node.

Formally, a graph G is defined to be a pair $[N(G), E(G)]$, where $N(G)$ is a non-empty finite set of elements called nodes, and $E(G)$ is a finite family of *unordered* pairs of elements of $N(G)$ called edges. $N(G)$ is called the 'node-set', and $E(G)$ the 'edge-family' of G. For computer graphics, it is very convenient to think of the node-set as an array of cartesian coordinates. Similarly, the edge-family becomes a two-column array of integers, the two integers in a row representing the end-nodes of an edge. In this chapter and others, this two-column array of integers is referred to as the 'connectivity matrix'.

Notice the *underlining* of 'unordered' in the above paragraph. For practical computer graphics (e.g. Inside/Outside tests – Chapter 4) it is often necessary to have edges arranged in a certain order. A 'directed graph' or 'digraph' I is defined to be a pair $[N(I), D(I)]$, where $N(I)$ is a non-empty finite set of elements called nodes, and $D(I)$ is a finite family of *ordered* pairs of elements of $N(I)$ called 'di-edges'. A di-edge whose first element is v and whose second element is w is called a di-edge from v to w and is written vw. The di-edges vw and wv are different.

An edge-sequence is a finite sequence of edges of the form

$$n_0 n_1, n_1 n_2, \ldots, n_{m-1} n_m$$

An edge-sequence has the property that any two consecutive edges are either adjacent or identical. This property can be used to pre-process a connectivity matrix, and to sort it into the correct sequence for a subsequent graphics procedure. n_0 is called the 'initial' node and n_m the 'final' node of the edge-sequence. The number of edges in an edge-sequence is called its 'length'.

An edge-sequence in which all the edges are distinct is called a 'trail'. If, in addition, the nodes $n_0, \ldots, n_m$ are distinct (except, possibly, $n_0 = n_m$), then the trail is called a 'path'. A path or trail is 'closed' if $n_0 = n_m$, and a closed path containing at least one edge is called a 'circuit'.

The concept of a circuit occurs several times in the following chapters.

3.2 **Types of 2D shapes**

In Chapter 2, we looked at some relationships between points (nodes in Graph Theory) and lines (edges in Graph Theory). For computer graphics applications, 2-dimensional objects are built by concatenating lines in a meaningful manner. The resulting 2D objects have position and area. The area may be bounded by many straight lines, or by a combination of straight lines and curves, such as conic sections, Bézier curves, etc.

From such bounded areas, it is possible to model 3D objects. One modelling technique is to describe a series of adjacent cross-sections, together with an expression that defines how the solid is interpolated from one section to the next. One of the simplest such solids is a cone, every section parallel to the base of which is a circle; the radius of the circle varies linearly from maximum at the base to zero at the apex.

One of the most complex (and macabre) is *The Visual Man* (available at web site **www.visualman.com/dataexpress/man.htm**). The man who donated his body was a murderer, sentenced to death in Texas. After unsuccessful appeals to higher U.S. courts, he was executed, his body was frozen, and then cut into slices 1 mm thick. After high-resolution scanning, expert analysis, and labelling, the cross-sectional images have been made available on compact discs for use by medical students, anatomists, surgeons, etc. The above web site is a demonstration of the package, and contains 188 images at 1 cm spacing.

Look at the two solid objects in Fig. 3.3 and imagine what would happen if you sawed horizontally through them. In a later chapter we consider how the cross-sectional shape is computed by intersecting the solid model with a horizontal plane, but for now just try to picture the effect of a saw cut.

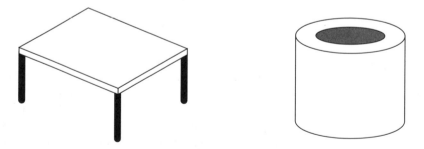

Figure 3.3 A 4-legged table and a length of piping.

The table object would give you four distinct squares. The pipe cross-section is two concentric circles. These are shown in Fig. 3.4.

Figure 3.4 illustrates the important concept of 'disjointedness'. The four squares are disjoint because they do not intersect one another. The two circles

Figure 3.4 Sections through 4-legged table and a length of piping.

are disjoint because, although one is inside the other, they do not intersect. Each of the squares is a circuit comprising four finite lines (edges). Each of the circles is a circuit, and is a complete 360° circular arc. Common sense tells us that the two circuits shown in Fig. 3.5 cannot be a cross-section through a solid object: they fail the test of disjointedness.

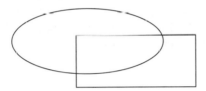

Figure 3.5 Non-disjoint circuits.

Next, we examine how circuits of straight lines may be stored in a simple data structure. Figure 3.6 shows an L-shaped outer circuit with a triangular hole.

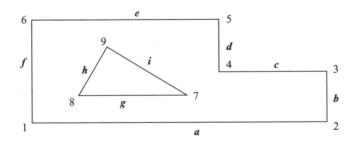

Figure 3.6 Simple 2-circuit section.

Each point (or node) is numbered and the coordinates of the points are stored in the 'geometry' array at the left of Fig. 3.7. Non-integer values have been selected, as the graphics programmer rarely has the luxury of being able to use integer arithmetic. The array on the right has been dubbed the 'connectivity' array, and stores the start and finish point for each line.

Node No.	X	Y	Line	Start	Finish
1	0.5	0.5	a	1	2
2	3.1	0.5	b	2	3
3	3.1	1.5	c	3	4
4	2.2	1.5	d	4	5
5	2.2	2.3	e	5	6
6	0.5	2.3	f	6	1
7	1.7	1.3	g	7	8
8	0.9	1.2	h	8	9
9	1.3	1.9	i	9	7

Figure 3.7 Geometry and connectivity arrays for Fig 3.6.

The line shown in the connectivity array separates the two distinct circuits. Of course, when processing the array stored in computer memory, it is necessary to check if a circuit has been completed by comparing the start point of the current circuit with the finish point of the current edge. The above data structure is an efficient method of storage, and there is little point in having a more complex one merely to distinguish between the circuits. The solution is to pre-process the data to find where each circuit begins. Hence, the array shown in Fig. 3.8 facilitates processing the entire shape.

Circuit No.	Start Point of Circuit	
1	1	*(Circuit 1 ends one before Circuit 2)*
2	7	*(Last circuit ends at highest numbered)*

Figure 3.8 Circuits extracted from the connectivity array.

In Chapter 2, we looked at methods to compute and validate the intersection of two finite lines. These are essential tools for checking that circuits are disjoint. From a visual examination of the shape, it is obvious that the two circuits are disjoint, and hence this is a valid cross-section of a solid object. Any computations carried out on such an object (e.g. to find the cross-sectional area) are simplified if the lines are treated as vectors (the edges are di-edges) and we adopt a convention whereby the direction indicates the INSIDE of the object.

The rule that will be adopted is:

> **The INSIDE is to the left of the vector**

Notice in Fig. 3.6 that the outer circuit runs (mainly) in an anticlockwise direction, whereas the inner circuit (which is a hole) runs clockwise. It is important always to bear in mind that '*INSIDE is to the left*' is the convention. It is *not* 'anticlockwise circuits are outer boundaries', or even 'clockwise circuits are holes'. The convention can be applied to any type of boundary structure used in computer graphics; the circuits do *not* have to consist entirely of straight lines.

3.3 Transformation of shapes

A 2D shape may be transformed in three basic ways:

1. translation
2. scaling
3. rotation.

The transformation of translation is illustrated in Fig. 3.9.

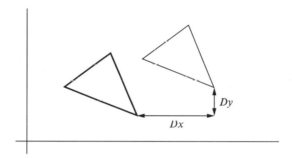

Figure 3.9 Translation.

Notice that every node in the untransformed shape is moved by Dx horizontally and by Dy vertically. As all vertices are subject to the same process, we express transformations simply in terms of their effect on a single node. The nomenclature used is that a point **P** with homogeneous coordinates

$$[x \quad y \quad 1]$$

becomes transformed to point **P'** with coordinates

$$[x' \quad y' \quad 1]$$

For translation

$$x' = x + Dx \quad \text{and} \quad y' = y + Dy$$

Hence

$$\mathbf{P'} = [x + Dx \quad y + Dy \quad 1].$$

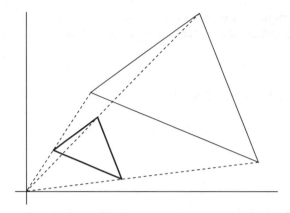

Figure 3.10 Scaling.

For **scaling**, the scale factor may be less than or greater than one, and need not be the same in the x and y directions. Notice that, as shown in Fig. 3.10, if the x and y scale factors have an *equal* value which is greater than one, then three effects can be observed:

- the proportions of the 2D shape remain the same,
- the shape is enlarged,
- the shape moves further from the origin.

Hence

$$\mathbf{P'} = [xS_x \quad yS_y \quad 1].$$

For **rotation** around the z axis, suppose that point $\mathbf{P}$ has polar coordinates (r, θ), as illustrated in Fig. 3.11.

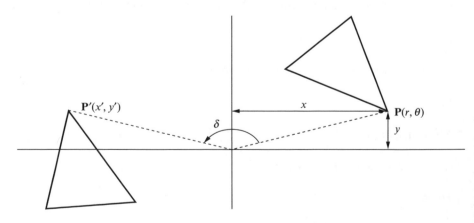

Figure 3.11 Rotation around z axis.

Hence: $x = r \cos \theta$ and $y = r \sin \theta$.
   When the point is rotated through angle δ

$$x' = r \cos(\theta + \delta)$$
$$y' = r \sin(\theta + \delta)$$

Expanding, using compound angle formulae

$$x' = r \cos \theta \cos \delta - r \sin \theta \sin \delta$$
$$y' = r \cos \theta \sin \delta + r \sin \theta \cos \delta.$$

Substituting the equations for the values of x and y:

$$x' = x \cos \delta - y \sin \delta$$
$$y' - x \sin \delta + y \cos \delta$$

Hence

$$P' = [x \cos \delta - y \sin \delta \quad x \sin \delta + y \cos \delta \quad 1]$$

For computing convenience, a 3×3 transformation matrix is created in which the appropriate elements are stored. The untransformed row vector is multiplied by the 3×3 matrix in order to transform it. Matrix multiplication has this general rule:

$$[x \quad y \quad 1] \begin{bmatrix} a_1 & b_1 & c_1 \\ a_2 & b_2 & c_2 \\ a_3 & b_3 & c_3 \end{bmatrix} = [a_1x + a_2y + a_3 \quad b_1x + b_2y + b_3 \quad c_1x + c_2y + c_3]$$

Hence, for translation the transformation matrix is:

$$\begin{bmatrix} 1 & 0 & 0 \\ 0 & 1 & 0 \\ Dx & Dy & 1 \end{bmatrix}$$

For scaling, the transformation matrix is:

$$\begin{bmatrix} S_x & 0 & 0 \\ 0 & S_y & 0 \\ 0 & 0 & 1 \end{bmatrix}$$

For rotation around the z axis through angle δ, the transformation matrix is:

$$\begin{bmatrix} \cos\delta & \sin\delta & 0 \\ -\sin\delta & \cos\delta & 0 \\ 0 & 0 & 1 \end{bmatrix}$$

Two other transformations are frequently used.

1. Reflect or flip about y axis: $x' = -x$; $y' = y$. Hence $Dx = -2x$ and so the transformation matrix is

$$\begin{bmatrix} 1 & 0 & 0 \\ 0 & 1 & 0 \\ -2x & 0 & 1 \end{bmatrix}$$

2. Reflect or flip about x axis: $x' = x$; $y' = -y$. Hence $Dy = -2y$ and so the transformation matrix is

$$\begin{bmatrix} 1 & 0 & 0 \\ 0 & 1 & 0 \\ 0 & -2y & 1 \end{bmatrix}$$

3.4 Summary

- In order to generalise much of the material presented in later chapters, some useful concepts from Graph Theory have been presented. In particular, the concept of a digraph as a 3D cross section is vital.
- A digraph that models the cross-section of a solid object may comprise one or more circuits. If there are multiple circuits then they must be disjoint.
- One possible data structure for line polygons comprises a Geometry array, and a Connectivity array. The first array gives the cartesian coordinates of the vertices, while the second array lists pairs of vertices that are connected by edges.
- For such a data structure to model a 3D cross-section, the ordering of the edges must be such that the inside of the shape is to the left of the edge vector.
- Shapes can be subjected to the transformations of Translation, Scaling, and Rotation. It is convenient to use a Transformation matrix to carry out the computation.

3.5 **Further reading**

Barton, E. E. and I. Buchanan, 'The Polygon Package', *Computer Aided Design*, Vol. 12, No. 1, pp. 3–11, 1965. The authors define a 'sheet' as a set of points enclosed by an ordered ring of alternating nodes and edges. This is slightly at odds with the Graph Theory approach used in this chapter, but amounts to the same thing.

Eastman, C. M. and K. Preiss, 'A review of solid shape modelling based on integrity verification', *Computer Aided Design*, Vol. 16, No. 2, pp. 66–80, 1984. One of the earliest papers that investigates how a set of data can be validated as a geometric model. They define the useful criterion of the 'orientability condition': an orientable surface allows recognition of its solid and non-solid sides.

Klein, F., *Geometry: Elementary Mathematics from an Advanced Standpoint*, Dover, 1939. There is much here about homogeneous coordinates in 2D and 3D. Mobius' Law (a surface has a solid and non-solid side) is treated.

Richardson, M., *Practical Computer Graphics*, McGraw-Hill Publishing Company, 1999. A general overview of computer graphics with an emphasis on practical applications.

Exercises

1. Convert Fig. 2.1 to a simple graph of nodes and edges. How many 1-nodes? How many 2-nodes? How many 3-nodes? Are there any circuits? If so, list the nodes on each circuit.
2. Is Fig. 2.1 a simple graph?
3. There are two triangles. The first has vertices at $(0, 0)$, $(8, 0)$, $(8, 6)$. The second has vertices at $(5, 3)$, $(7, 3)$, $(5, 1)$. On paper, compute the intersections of each line from the first triangle with each line from the second and check if the intersection is valid. How many valid intersections do you get? What does this imply about the disjointedness of the two triangles? When you have a theoretical answer, plot the triangles on grid paper as a check.
4. With a pocket calculator, using a transformation matrix, scale a triangle with vertices at $(5, 3)$, $(7, 3)$, $(5, 1)$ by 2.0 in the x direction and by 0.5 in the y direction. What is the difference in area between the transformed and un-transformed triangles?
5. With a pocket calculator, using a transformation matrix, rotate a triangle with vertices at $(6, 2)$, $(8, 3)$, $(5, -1)$ through $-45°$ around the z axis. Plot the result on grid paper and check by using compasses to rotate a plot of the un-transformed shape.

CHAPTER 4

Processing 2D shapes

4.1 Introduction

An image stored in a computer (either as a graph or a bitmap) may often serve one or more of the following purposes:

- to represent a cross-section or a surface of a solid object (e.g. an engineering drawing),
- to represent a logical process precisely (e.g. a flow chart),
- to illustrate a process or a plan,
- to present the human eye/brain system with something that it can recognise and interpret,
- to be attractive and/or interesting to look at.

In this chapter, we look at some useful processes that can be carried out on digraphs. Firstly, we look at a test that has wide applications in geometric modelling, topology, cartography, and surveying. An Inside/Outside testing procedure is a 'must' when we need to determine if a point lies within a particular boundary, no matter whether that boundary is a solid section, a piece of land or a political or geographical boundary.

Secondly, we look at Boolean operations on two non-disjoint boundaries. This process is essential for geometric modelling and computer-aided manufacture. Thirdly, we examine the process known as 'inflation'. The inflation of a 2D boundary is a new boundary, every point on which is the same distance from the original boundary. The ability to generate such an inflated boundary automatically is vital in applications such as the design of printed circuit boards, and in cutting processes when a significant amount of material is removed.

Lastly, we look at how the geometric properties (area, centroid, second moment of area, etc.) of a shape can be computed. This, of course, is particularly useful in engineering analysis.

4.2 Inside/outside tests

In Chapter 3 we looked mainly at those 2D shapes, that are cross-sections of a 3D object. We will now examine two algorithms that will compute whether a

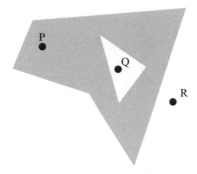

Figure 4.1 Only point **P** is inside the boundary of the object.

point is inside the boundary of the shape. Look at Fig. 4.1 and the three points **P, Q, R**.

To the human eye–brain system it is apparent that **P** is inside, **Q** is outside (in a hole), and **R** is outside. It is unprofitable to consider how humans are able to recognise instantly if a point is inside or outside a boundary, as it leads to all the complexities of robot vision: a topic that is completely outside the scope of this book. Fortunately for progress in computer graphics, it was discovered early on that there are two logical processes that can reach the correct conclusion, albeit not so rapidly as the human brain.

4.2.1 *Half-line test*

The Half-line Test has the advantage of *not* requiring the data to be sorted into circuits of contiguous edges, although of course it must be *capable* of being thus sorted as it must represent a bounded area. It is often the case that data are generated by a user who creates vertices, and joins them together in some creative manner. With a half-line test, the only pre-processing of the data that is required is to check for disjoint circuits. The half-line test *has* to be used if the shape is not built entirely from straight lines; the 'surroundedness' test cannot be applied. Unfortunately, these are the only advantages of the half-line test: it is very complicated to implement because of the large number of exceptions that can arise.

Figure 4.2 is based upon Fig. 4.1, with the addition of horizontal lines extended horizontally from points **P, Q, R** to some infinitely far point to the right.

Notice that the half-line from **P** intersects the bounding edges three times. From **Q**, there are two intersections, and from **R**, there are none. Generalising, if there is an *odd* number of intersections then the point is *inside* the 2D boundary.

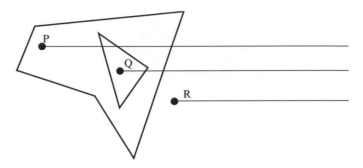

Figure 4.2 Half-lines from three test points.

If further explanation of this logic is required, then consider what occurs at an intersection – a jump from one side of the boundary to the other. As the half-line goes to infinity, it always ends *outside* the boundary. Hence, an *odd* number of boundary crossings proves that the point at the start of the half-line is *inside* the boundary.

OUTLINE ALGORITHM

1. Set INSIDE = false
2. Set COUNT = 0
3. Set THISEDGE = 1 (the current edge)
4. Compute where the half-line intersects the current edge.
5. If the intersection lies between the ends of the current edge *and* the X value is greater than the *x* coordinate of the test point, then increment COUNT. Use the *t* parameter to check former condition – see page 22.
6. Increment THISEDGE.
7. If THISEDGE is less than or equal to the total number of edges, then go to step 4.
8. If COUNT is an odd number then set INSIDE = true.

~~~

4.2.2 *Surroundedness test*

This test can be conveniently illustrated by the reader, using simple materials such as a corkboard, string, and drawing pins. One end of the string is fixed to test point **P** in Fig. 4.3.

At vertex No. 1, with the string taut, mark the line **P1**. That line is the initial angular position. Keeping the string taught, move along each vector in turn and keep a record of the approximate angle turned through *from the initial position*. Notice that this cumulative angle temporarily decreases sometimes,

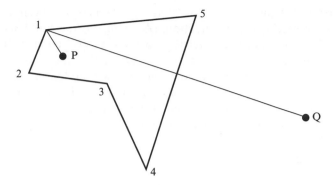

Figure 4.3 A practical demonstration of 'surroundedness' test.

and then increases until, back at vertex No. 1, it reaches the full 360° in the anticlockwise (positive) direction.

Now go through the same process, based upon point **Q**. The cumulative angle mainly increases until you reach vertex No. 4, and then it diminishes to zero. Hence, a cumulative angle of +360° indicates that the test point is *inside* the boundary. Is this true for more complicated boundaries, with several circuits, including holes? In the absence of a rigorous proof, it is suggested that the reader invent the most complicated set of disjoint circuits you care to, and test it as before. When you have followed around one complete circuit, note the accumulated angle, and do not change it when you switch to the start of a new circuit. Once the new circuit is under way, the angle accumulation continues.

If your test point is inside a hole, then you will notice that the accumulated angle decreases by 360° when traversing the circuit that bounds the hole. This explains the logic behind the convention that 'inside' is to the left of the vector. It ensures that a point surrounded by material will produce an accumulated angle of +360°, whereas a point surrounded by a hole will accumulate −360°. The result of surroundedness test computations can never be −360°, as a hole cannot exist in isolation: it must be a hole in something.

When implementing this paradigm, it is important *not* to make a mistake to which novice programmers are prone when working with angular measurements. A constant called TwoPi holds the equivalent of 360° in radians. A Boolean variable Inside and a real variable TotalAngle have been declared; the accumulated angle is stored in the latter. A typical fragment of bad C++ code would be:

```
bool Inside = false;

if (TotalAngle == TwoPi)
  Inside = true;
```

With pins and string, you can see that `TotalAngle` has been accumulated from at least three changes of direction. (A triangle is the simplest 2D shape.) More typically, there are many vertices forming several circuits. It would be astounding if the cumulative result were *exactly* 2π to the number of decimal places in machine memory. It would be equally astounding if the cumulative result were exactly zero. An appropriate threshold to distinguish between the two cases might be 3.0, a whole number at about mid-range, approximating to π. Hence, a practicable C++ encoding would be:

```
bool Inside = false;

if (TotalAngle > 3.0)
   Inside = true;
```

4.3 **Boolean operations on 2D shapes**

Two digraphs represent non-disjoint boundaries A and B. They are shown in Fig. 4.4.

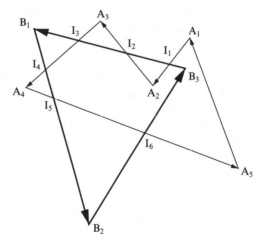

Figure 4.4 Combination of two boundaries.

The UNION of A and B (**A ∪ B**) is defined as the boundary which contains all the material that lies inside A, *or* lies inside B, *or* is inside both A and B. In other words, UNION is like the INCLUSIVE OR operation of Boolean algebra.

To find the boundary **A ∪ B** we start at a point on A such as A_1 and proceed along vector A_1A_2 until either A_2 is reached or, as in this example, the boundary of B is intersected at I_1. Having met an intersection, we move to boundary B and proceed in the vector direction until intersection I_2 is found.

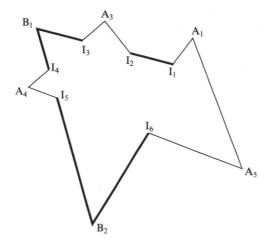

Figure 4.5 Union of A and B (**A** ∩ **B**).

From I_2, it is possible to move to A_3 without encountering an intersection. The same set of rules is followed until the new circuit closes at the starting point giving the boundary $A_1I_1I_2A_3I_3B_1I_4A_4I_5B_2I_6A_5A_1$ shown in Fig. 4.5

Notice that the union boundary could start at B_1 or B_2. It could *not* start at B_3, as that vertex is *inside* Λ.

The INTERSECTION of A and B (**A** ∩ **B**) is defined as the boundary which contains all the material that lies within both A AND B. In other words, intersection is like the AND operation of Boolean algebra. This time it is *essential* to find a starting point that is either on the boundary of both A and B, or inside both A and B. B_3 is suitable, but B_1 and B_2 are not. Hence, the intersection (shown in Fig. 4.6) is boundary $B_3I_1A_2I_2I_3I_4I_5\ I_6B_3$.

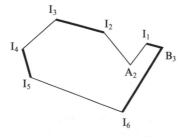

Figure 4.6 Intersection of A and B (**A** ∩ **B**).

The DIFFERENCE of A and B (**A** − **B**) is defined as the boundary which contains all the material that lies within A AND NOT within B. In other words, DIFFERENCE is like the AND NOT operation from Boolean algebra. A good analogy is to think of A as a piece of rolled-out pastry and think of boundary B as a pastry cutter. When the cutter has been pressed into A then what remains is pastry that did not lie within the boundary of B.

As may be seen in Fig. 4.7, it is essential to start at a point that *does not* lie on B. A_1 would be suitable.

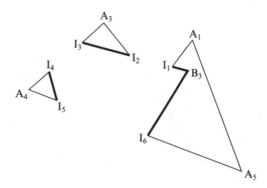

Figure 4.7 Difference of B from A (**A** − **B**).

This time, the result of 'cutting' away shape B is to create three disjoint circuits

$$A_1I_1B_3I_6A_5A_1 \quad A_3I_3I_2A_3 \quad A_4I_5I_4A_4$$

Notice that, as soon as the first intersection point is reached at I_1, the boundary is generated by moving in the *opposite* direction to the intersected vector. This produces new edge I_1B_1, so the rule to be applied is that *differenced* edges are followed *counter* to the vector direction. This would appear to be common sense (with reference to the pastry cutter analogy). Material is being *removed from* (rather than added to) shape A. Hence, we may say that following edges in the vector direction *adds* material whereas the counter direction *removes* material.

4.4 **Inflation and deflation**

Another very useful operation that can be performed on a 2D cross-section is termed 'inflation'. The inflation B of a boundary A can be defined as the shape which is everywhere a fixed distance (called the offset) away from boundary A. Hence, if a point is on or outside B its *minimum* distance from shape A is the offset distance. There are several manufacturing operations where it is vital to maintain a minimum distance from a shape. For example, there must be a minimum clearance between the copper conducting parts of a printed circuit board in order to minimise the possibility of sparks jumping between conductors.

Deflation is the exact opposite of inflation: all points on the deflation boundary are an equal distance *inside* the boundary. The shape shown in Fig. 4.8 is represented inside the computer as a digraph, hence the vector arrows. It has an outer boundary with both convex and concave corners; the hole also has both types of corner. The process of inflation will be illustrated step by step.

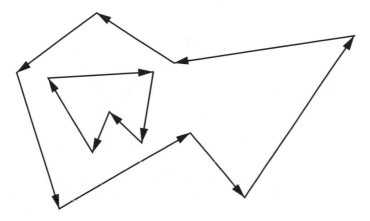

Figure 4.8 Boundary to be inflated.

Step 1 is to create a new vector *parallel* to the original and offset to the *right* of the vector direction. (In the case of deflation, the offset is to the left of the vector.) This step is illustrated in Fig. 4.9.

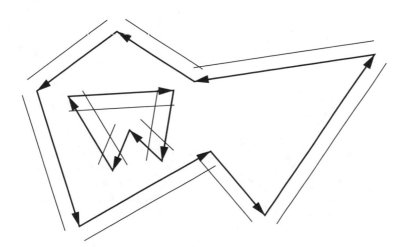

Figure 4.9 Inflation – step 1 – offset vectors.

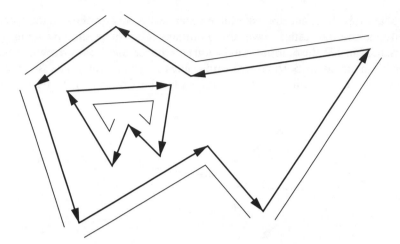

Figure 4.10 Inflation – step 2 – truncate at concave corners.

Step 2 is to deal with *concave* corners. These are corners when the change of vector direction is *clockwise* and the offset vectors *intersect*. Each such vector is truncated to create the correct offset concave corner. The intersection is computed from the homogeneous coordinates of the offset lines. The first offset vector finishes at this intersection point, and the second begins there. The results of this truncation are illustrated in Fig. 4.10.

The final step is to deal with *convex* corners. In Fig. 4.10, there is a gap between the offset vectors, that is filled in Fig. 4.11 by a circular arc whose centre is at the original corner, and whose radius equals the offset. The angle at each end of the arc is the direction of the adjacent vector *minus* 90°.

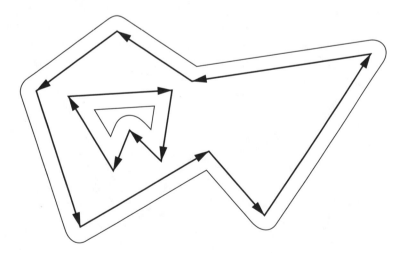

Figure 4.11 Inflation – final step – arc at convex corners.

At first sight, the mechanics of inflation/deflation appear quite simple, but after the above three steps have been completed, it is necessary to validate the result. Figure 4.12 shows a large inflation of Fig. 4.8 and it may be seen that the inflation of the hole is a self-intersecting shape.

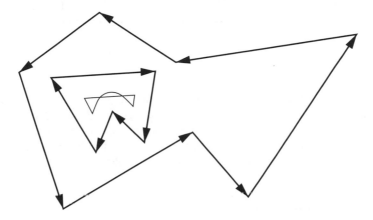

Figure 4.12 Excessive inflation.

The self-intersection can be eliminated by clipping the offset vectors. In the above example, the result would be two triangles. However, there is a limit to this process and eventually the offset of the hole will vanish completely. The algorithm to deal with self-intersection is complex, as it has to deal with many special cases.

In manufacturing practice, the 2D boundaries that require computation of an inflated shape are not confined to line polygons. A concave corner is a weak feature of a solid object, as the material could be highly stressed there, and a crack can easily start and grow. Therefore, designers will generally eliminate a region of high stress by inserting a 'fillet radius' instead of a sharp corner. Such a fillet is shown in Fig. 4.13. Hence, it is common for the outline of manufactured articles to be a line/arc polygon.

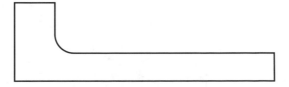

Figure 4.13 A line/arc polygon.

The inflation of a fillet (concave) arc is a concentric circle with a radius equal to the original radius minus the offset. The start and finish angles of the offset are the same as those of the original. The complete inflation is shown in Fig. 4.14.

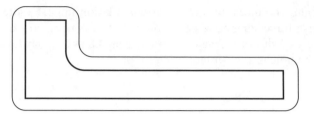

Figure 4.14 Inflation of a line/arc polygon.

If the inflation offset is excessive then the fillet arc will be the first feature to be eliminated when the offset exceeds the radius of the fillet. If the offset exceeds the radius of the arc then the tangent lines must be truncated. This is yet another example of how complex an inflation algorithm needs to be in order to determine the correct boundary for all possible offsets.

4.5 **Geometric properties**

Figure 4.15 shows a polygon as a digraph. If the coordinates of the start of an edge are (x_i, y_i) and the coordinates of the finish are (x_j, y_j), then for each edge an element area a and an element centroid, (c_1, c_2) are computed from the following equations:

$$a = (x_i y_j - x_j y_i)/2$$
$$c_1 = (x_i + x_j)/3$$
$$c_2 = (y_i + y_j)/3$$

For each circuit, the following summations are required.

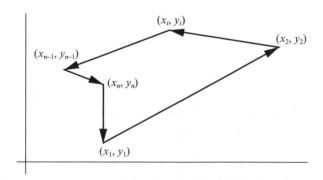

Figure 4.15 Computing geometric properties.

If there are n vertices in the circuit, labelled $1...n$, then the ith value of a is $(x_iy_j - x_jy_i)/2$, where $j = i \bmod n + 1$

$$A = \Sigma a \hspace{6cm} Area$$

$$M_1 = \Sigma ac_2 \hspace{4.5cm} Moment\ of\ Area\ about\ x\ axis$$

$$M_2 = \Sigma ac_1 \hspace{4.5cm} Moment\ of\ Area\ about\ y\ axis$$

$$R_1 = \Sigma a(y_i^2 + y_j^2 + y_iy_j)/6 \hspace{2cm} Second\ Moment\ of\ Area\ about\ x\ axis$$

$$R_2 = \Sigma a(x_i^2 + x_j^2 + x_ix_j)/6 \hspace{2cm} Second\ Moment\ of\ Area\ about\ y\ axis$$

$$R_3 = \Sigma a(x_iy_i + x_jy_j + (x_iy_j + x_jy_i)/2)/6 \hspace{1cm} Principal\ Second\ Moment\ of\ Area$$

All of the above summations must be done in vector order, and each circuit must be summed back to the start vertex.

Example 4.1

Plot the following shape on grid paper. The arrays model a rectangle with a rectangular hole. The outer rectangle measures 300 mm by 200 mm, so obviously its area is 60,000 mm². The inner rectangle measures 200 mm by 100 mm, so its area is 20,000 mm². Clearly, the net area is 40,000 mm² and we will now check this.

	Geometry	Array	Connectivity	Array
1	0	0	1	2
2	300	0	2	3
3	300	200	3	4
4	0	200	4	1
5	50	50	5	6
6	50	150	6	7
7	250	150	7	8
8	250	50	8	5

For the outer rectangle:

$$A_1 = (0 - 0)/2 + (60000 - 0)/2 + (60000 - 0)/2 + (0 - 0)/2$$

$$= 60000\ check$$

For the inner rectangle:

$$A_2 = (7500 - 2500)/2 + (7500 - 37500)/2 + (12500 - 37500)/2$$

$$+ (12500 - 2500)/2 = -20000\ check$$

Hence, the net area is $60000 - 20000 = 40000$

As the rectangles are concentric, the centroid should be at (150, 100).

For the outer rectangle:

$$M_2 = 0(0 + 300)/3 + 30000(300 + 300)/3 + 30000(300 + 0)/3 + 0(0 + 0)/3$$
$$= 9000000$$
$$M_1 = 0(0 + 0)/3 + 30000(0 + 200)/3 + 30000(200 + 200)/3 + 0(200 + 0)/3$$
$$= 6000000$$

For the inner rectangle:

$$M_2 = 2500(50 + 50)/3 - 15000(50 + 250)/3 - 12500(250 + 250)/3$$
$$+ 5000(250 + 50)/3$$
$$= -3000000$$
$$M_1 = 2500(50 + 150)/3 - 15000(150 + 150)/3 - 12500(150 + 50)/3$$
$$+ 5000(50 + 50)/3$$
$$= -2000000$$

Hence, the net value of M_2 is 9000000 − 3000000 = 6000000 and so the distance of the centroid from the y axis is 6000000/40000 = 150 mm   *check*
Similarly, the net value of M_1 is 6000000 − 2000000 = 4000000 and so the distance of the centroid from the x axis is 4000000/40000 = 100 mm   *check*.
The computation of the geometric properties of a cross-section is provided as a utility in many computer-aided drafting and computer-aided design software packages. Generally, the shape will already appear on the graphics display and when the position of the centroid has been computed, it is indicated by the automatic insertion of two perpendicular chain lines. A full list of properties may either be displayed or printed out. The second moments of area are of interest to structural engineers who need to compute how a component will deflect when subjected to certain loads.

4.6 Summary

- A 3D cross-section modelled as a digraph can be processed in order to yield several valuable results.
- Two ways of testing if a point lies inside or outside a boundary have been examined. The only pre-processing required for the 'half-line' test is a check that multiple circuits are disjoint. However, this paradigm often fails when the half-line passes through a vertex. The 'surroundedness' test must

have the data in the form of a digraph, and thereafter the implementation is not difficult.

- Complex 3D cross-sections can be built by carrying out Boolean operations on less complex circuits. The processes for union, intersection, and difference have been presented. This material is referred to in Chapter 8 when we examine the solid modelling technique called Constructive Solid Geometry (CSG).
- The important process of inflation has been treated in detail, and attention has been drawn to the complexities that arise when the offset is excessive.
- The geometric properties of a 3D cross-section built entirely from straight lines are readily computed using summation formulae.

4.7 **Further reading**

The half-line test is used in GKS, and details of some inside/outside tests appear in books on Computational Geometry. It is difficult to discover books and papers for some of the other material in this chapter. For example, the author is not aware of a practicable inflation algorithm that has been published. The following would provide additional material for the other topics discussed in this chapter.

Brodlie, K. W. (Editor), *Mathematical Methods in Computer Graphics and Design*, Academic Press, London, 1980. There are numerous citations to papers that deal with Boolean operations in relation to constructive solid geometry. The treatment in this chapter was written entirely from the author's experience of consulting work in CAD.

Hill, F. S. *Computer Graphics*, Collier Macmillan, London 1990. One of the few books on the subject that examines how the area of a polygon may be computed. The treatment (vector cross product) is more theoretical than in this chapter, but some other general results may be of interest to the reader.

Klein, F., *Geometry: Elementary Mathematics from an Advanced Standpoint*, Dover, 1939. Klein generally has some answers to questions on geometrical procedures.

Laszlo, M., *Computational Geometry and Computer Graphics in C++*, Prentice Hall, 1995. Practical solutions to basic problems in computational geometry.

O'Rourke, J., *Computational Geometry in C*, Cambridge University Press, 1998.

Exercises

1. A shape has vertces on an outer boundary at $(0, 0)$, $(6, 6)$, $(5, 7)$, $(1, 3)$, $(-1, 5)$, and $(-3, 3)$. There is a hole with vertices at $(0, 1)$, $(1, 2)$, $(-1, 4)$ and $(-3, 3)$. Compute the number of times that a half-line to the right from a point **P** at $(-1, 3.5)$ intersects the shape. What does your result imply about point **P**?

2. Arrange the edge vectors specified in question 1 so that both the outer boundary and the hole abide by the convention. Then, determine the cumulative angle subtended at point **Q** (2, 3) by the shape. What does your result imply about point **Q**?

3. What is the largest inflation that could be applied to the shape in question 1 before self-intersection occurs?

4. Find the area, the centroid, and the second moments of area of a polygon having vertices (0, 0), (4, 0), (3, 2), (6, 3), and (0, 8). Check that you get the same answer using:
   - a pocket calculator,
   - a spreadsheet,
   - a simple C program that you have written in which the five pairs of co-ordinates are stored in a suitable constant array.

CHAPTER 5

Curves

5.1 **Parametric cubic curves**

Historically, a 'spline' was a flexible strip of metal used by draftsmen to produce a smooth curve through a designated set of points. Several small weights were distributed along the length of the strip to hold it in position on the drawing board as the 'spline curve' was drawn. It may be shown that a strip of metal loaded in this way is not just one cubic curve, but a series of curve sections blended together with the first and second derivatives continuous across adjacent sections. Hence, there is no change in the radius of curvature between sections.

A spline curve is specified by a set of coordinates (called control points) that indicate the general shape of the curve. These control points can then be fitted with piecewise continuous polynomial functions in two ways:

1. A curve that passes through each control point. The resulting curve is said to 'interpolate' the set of control points.
2. A curve that only passes through the end-points. The other control points exert a 'pull', and the curve is said to 'approximate' the set of control points.

A designer can be offered two different types of operation. In both cases it is necessary to specify the end-points of the curve and some intermediate points. An **interpolate** operation will result in the curve passing through the intermediate points, whereas with an **approximate** operation the intermediate points will simply have some influence on the shape of the curve.

Up until this chapter, we have been concerned with 2D shapes composed almost exclusively of straight lines. In Chapter 2, we looked at the circular arc, which is a simple curve widely found in manufactured articles, especially those formed by cutting metal. The circular arc imposes serious restrictions on creative and engineering design. For example, a modern car body or an aircraft wing cannot be manufactured from straight lines and circular arcs.

Of course, a straight line is linear in both the common and the mathematical sense. On page 22 it is stated that the parametric form of a straight line is:

$$x = X_0(1 - t) + X_1 t$$
$$y = Y_0(1 - t) + Y_1 t$$

These equations can be rearranged as

$$x = X_0 + (X_1 - X_0)t$$
$$y = Y_0 + (Y_1 - Y_0)t$$

The parameter t varies from 0 at (X_0, Y_0) to 1 at (X_1, Y_1), and it is a very useful measure of how far a point on the curve is from one end. The general form of the above equations is:

$$x = a_0 + a_1 t$$
$$y = b_0 + b_1 t$$

If we introduce a third coefficient and raise t to the power 2, we get a parametric quadratic curve:

$$x = a_0 + a_1 t + a_2 t^2$$
$$y = b_0 + b_1 t + b_2 t^2$$

Such a curve can be used to interpolate the set of control points, but it is of little use to creative and engineering designers. This is because only the first derivative is continuous across adjacent sections. In other words, the adjacent sections have a common tangent, but there can be an abrupt change in the radius of curvature. Such a change neither looks good, nor is it conducive to a smooth fluid flow over a surface manufactured from such a curve.

By adding a fourth coefficient we get a **parametric cubic curve** that has most of the properties that designers require. The adjacent sections not only have a common tangent, but also a common radius of curvature.

$$x = a_0 + a_1 t + a_2 t^2 + a_3 t^3$$
$$y = b_0 + b_1 t + b_2 t^2 + b_3 t^3$$

Notice that there are eight (unknown) coefficients in the above equations. A designer using such curves will specify indirectly where a section of the curve starts and where it finishes – the values of x and y when $t = 0$ and $t = 1$. These data will yield the following equations:

$$x_0 = a_0$$
$$y_0 = b_0$$
$$x_1 = a_0 + a_1 + a_2 + a_3$$
$$y_1 = b_0 + b_1 + b_2 + b_3$$

We now have four equations, but eight unknowns. Hence, four more equations are needed in order to find all the coefficients. Most designers want to be able to control the gradient (or slope) of the curve at the end-points, but they do not want to have to specify it directly. In other words, the user of parametric cubic curves wants to be able to influence the following:

$dx/dt = a_1 + 2a_2t + 3a_3t^2$

$(a_1$ at $t = 0$; $a_1 + 2a_2 + 3a_3$ at $t = 1)$

$dy/dt = b_1 + 2b_2t + 3b_3t^2$

$(b_1$ at $t = 0$; $b_1 + 2b_2 + 3b_3$ at $t = 1)$

The influence over the curve is achieved via the intermediate points. dx/dt and dy/dt are not specified directly.

5.2 Bézier curves

One particularly useful form of parametric cubic is the Bézier curve, which runs from

$\mathbf{P_0} = (x_0, y_0)$ at $t = 0$

to

$\mathbf{P_3} = (x_3, y_3)$ at $t = 1$

and is influenced by control points

$\mathbf{P_1} = (x_1, y_1)$ and $\mathbf{P_2} = (x_2, y_2)$.

A typical Bézier curve is shown in Fig. 5.1.

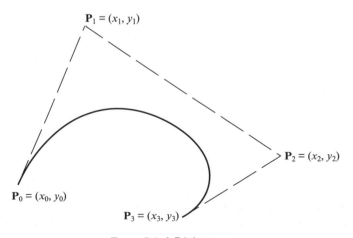

Figure 5.1 A Bézier curve.

You can observe how the curve passes through P_0 and P_3 by substituting values of 0 and 1 in these parametric equations:

$$x = x_0(1 - t)^3 + 3x_1(1 - t)^2 t + 3x_2(1 - t)t^2 + x_3 t^3$$

$$y = y_0(1 - t)^3 + 3y_1(1 - t)^2 t + 3y_2(1 - t)t^2 + y_3 t^3$$

At $t = 0$ and at $t = 1$ the coordinates of the control points P_1 and P_2 are multiplied by zero, and so they play no part in determining the *position* of the curve at its end points. What the control points do is to determine the initial and the final *gradient* of the curve.

In many computer graphics applications that facilitate the creation of parametric cubic curves, users find it most convenient to specify the end gradients of the curve *indirectly*. The Bézier curve has an initial gradient equal to the slope of line P_0P_1 and final gradient equal to that of P_2P_3. P_1 and P_2 are called 'control' points because they affect the shape of the curve, although it does not pass through them. Notice that the actual coordinates of the control points (x_1, y_1) and (x_2, y_2) are immaterial: what matters are the values of the *gradients*.

Differentiating the above equations, we get:

$$dx/dt = -3x_0(1 - t)^2 + 3x_1(1 - t)^2 - 6x_1(1 - t)t + 6x_2(1 - t)t^2 - 3x_2 t^2 + 3x_3 t^2$$

$$dy/dt = -3y_0(1 - t)^2 + 3y_1(1 - t)^2 - 6y_1(1 - t)t + 6y_2(1 - t)t^2 - 3y_2 t^2 + 3y_3 t^2$$

When $t = 0$

$$dx/dt = -3x_0 + 3x_1$$

$$dy/dt = -3y_0 + 3y_1$$

Hence, $dy/dx = (-3y_0 + 3y_1)/(-3x_0 + 3x_1) = (y_1 - y_0)/(x_1 - x_0)$.

In other words, the direction P_0P_1 is the gradient at the start of the Bézier curve.

Similarly, when $t = 1$

$$dx/dt = -3x_2 + 3x_3$$

$$dy/dt = -3y_2 + 3y_3$$

Hence, $dy/dx = (-3y_2 + 3y_3)/(-3x_2 + 3x_3) = (y_3 - y_2)/(x_3 - x_2)$

Thus, the direction P_2P_3 is the gradient at the finish of the Bézier curve.

The Bézier formulation is $x = x_0(1 - t)^3 + 3x_1(1 - t)^2 t + 3x_2(1 - t)t^2 + x_3 t^3$. Notice that each term contains

1. a binomial coefficient (symbol B will be used below),
2. the coordinate of a control point,
3. $(1 - t)$ raised to a power that decrements by 1 with each successive term,
4. t raised to a power that increments by 1 with each successive term.

Adding extra control points so that, with three control points in place, we have two Bézier curves seamlessly blended together, can considerably enhance the usefulness of this type of cubic curve. Four control points give three blended Bézier curves, etc. Hence, n points (including the two end-points) mathematically define $n–3$ blended Bézier curves. Only one equation is required for the complete set of curves, and its format is exactly as described above. The binomial series follows the triangular pattern described by Pascal:

$$
\begin{array}{ccccccccccccc}
& & & & & & 1 & & & & & & \\
& & & & & 1 & & 1 & & & & & \\
& & & & 1 & & 2 & & 1 & & & & \\
& & & 1 & & 3 & & 3 & & 1 & & & \text{(4 point Bézier)} \\
& & 1 & & 4 & & 6 & & 4 & & 1 & & \text{(5 point Bézier)} \\
& 1 & & 5 & & 10 & & 10 & & 5 & & 1 & \text{(6 point Bézier)} \\
& & & & & & & & & & & & \text{etc.}
\end{array}
$$

Hence, the x equation for a 5-point curve is

$$x = x_0(1 - t)^4 + 4x_1(1 - t)^3 t + 6x_2(1 - t)^2 t^2 + 4x_3(1 - t)t^3 + x_4 t^4$$

and for 6 points it is

$$x = x_0(1 - t)^5 + 5x_1(1 - t)^4 t + 10x_2(1 - t)^3 t^2 + 10x_2(1 - t)^2 t^3 + 5x_3(1 - t)t^4 + x_4 t^5$$

The first binomial coefficient (B_0) is always 1. For $n = 6$ points, B_1 can be obtained by multiplying B_0 by $(6 - 1)/1$ to give 5. Similarly, B_2 can be obtained by multiplying B_1 by $(6 - 2)/2$ to give 10. This gives us the general rule that

$$B_r = \frac{n - r}{r} B_{r-1}$$

Generally, the equation for x of an n-point curve is

$$x(t) = \sum_{r=0}^{n-1} B_r x_r (1 - t)^{n-r-1} t^r$$

The equation for y of an n-point curve is

$$y(t) = \sum_{r=0}^{n-1} B_r y_r (1 - t)^{n-r-1} t^r$$

Notice that there will be *n* coefficients formed from the product $B_r x_r$ and that they can be computed and stored before points on the curve are computed. The following C++ code shows the coefficients being computed first and then *t* is incremented in steps of 0.01. Consecutive points thus computed are connected together by drawing short straight lines between them.

```cpp
void DrawBezierCurve (int n, float x[16], float y[16])
{
  int B[16];
  int i, r;
  float Xcoeff[16], Ycoeff[16];
  float t, Xt, Yt, tToPowerR, tCompToPower;

  B[0] = 1;
  Xcoeff[0] = B[0] * x[0];
  Ycoeff[0] = B[0] * y[0];

  for (r = 1; r < n; r++)
    {
    B[r] = B[r - 1] * (n - r) / r;
    Xcoeff[r] = B[r] * x[r];
    Ycoeff[r] = B[r] * y[r];
    }
    /* move to x[0], y[0] */
  for (i = 1; i < 100; r++)
    {
    t = 0.01 * i;
    tToPowerR = 1;
    tCompToPower = 1 - t;
    for (r = 2; r < n; r++) tCompToPower = tCompToPower * (1 - t);
    Xt = 0.0;
    Yt = 0.0;

  for (r = 0; r < n; r++)
    {
    Xt = Xt + Xcoeff[r] * tToPowerR * tCompToPower;
    Yt = Yt + Ycoeff[r] * tToPowerR * tCompToPower;
    tToPowerR = tToPowerR * t;
    tCompToPower = tCompToPower / (1 - t);
    }

  /* plot Xt, Yt */
  }
}
```

Figure 5.2 was created using the above routine with 16 control points. A dashed line connects the control points. The arrow points to the final line; notice that it is tangential to the final point on the curve.

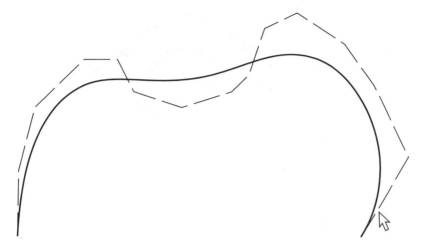

Figure 5.2 Bézier curve with 16 control points.

5.3 **Space curves**

2D Bézier curves are easily extended into three dimensions. We just add an expression for z anywhere along the curve. The general curve with n points has the equation

$$z(t) = \sum_{r=0}^{n-1} B_r z_r (1-t)^{n-r-1} t^r$$

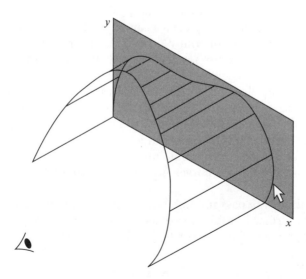

Figure 5.3 A space curve.

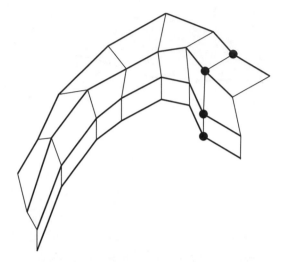

Figure 5.4 Control points for a Bézier surface.

Note that the three functions $x(t)$, $y(t)$, $z(t)$ together define a space *curve*, not a *curved surface*. A space curve is a curve along which the x, y, and z coordinates all vary, as opposed to a 2D curve (like that shown in Fig. 5.2), along which z is constant. The difference is illustrated in Fig. 5.3.

A viewer looking along the z axis (from where the eyeball is shown) would see the curve to which the arrow points. It is the space curve projected onto the x–y plane and is the same as Fig. 5.2. The space curve has its z coordinates indicated at 10% intervals and these z values vary all along the curve. When viewed along the z axis the variation of the z values cannot be detected.

Two sets of orthogonal Bézier curves can be used to design a curved surface by specifying an input mesh of control points. Such a mesh is shown in Fig. 5.4. There are eight control points for the first set of space curves and they are joined with a thick line. There are four control points for the second set, joined with a thin line. The eight points define a series of space curves along which parameter t varies from 0 to 1. In the orthogonal direction, it is necessary to have another parameter, and the symbol u will be used. The four points define a series of space curves along which parameter u varies from 0 to 1. Obviously, there is a total of $8 \times 4 = 32$ control points.

The four bounding space curves are readily computed, and are shown in Fig. 5.5.

A Bézier surface will pass through the four control points that bound it. Any point **P** on the surface is a function of both t and u and is computed by forming the vector product of the two orthogonal space curves:

$$\mathbf{P}(t, u) = \sum_{s=0}^{m-1} \sum_{r=0}^{n-1} \mathbf{p}_{(s,r)} B_s (1-u)^{m-s-1} u^s B_r (1-t)^{n-r-1} t^r$$

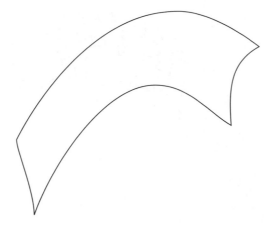

Figure 5.5 Bounding space curves for control points shown in Fig. 5.4.

The above summation requires some interpretation in order to implement a Bézier surface computer graphics procedure. The vector product of the two orthogonal space curves is computed by treating the u-parameter coefficients as a row vector, the control points as a column vector, and multiplying the two. The result can be treated as a new row vector that is then multiplied by a column vector that represents the t-parameter coefficients. There are four control points on the u curve, and eight on the t curve shown in Fig. 5.4. Hence in this case, the vector product is computed from the following multiplication:

$$[(1-u)^3 \quad 3u(1-u)^2 \quad 3u^2(1-u) \quad u^3] \cdot P_{(s,\,r)} \cdot \begin{bmatrix} (1-t)^7 \\ 7t(1-t)^6 \\ 21t^2(1-t)^5 \\ 35t^3(1-t)^4 \\ 35t^4(1-t)^3 \\ 21t^5(1-t)^2 \\ 7t^6(1-t) \\ t^7 \end{bmatrix}$$

It is possible to give the user of a computer-aided design package an impression of how the surface will appear by plotting one series of curves, each with a constant u value, and another set each with a constant t value. When the values of u and t have been set, the above row and column vectors are readily computed, then multiplied. The result is then multiplied by the values of x, y and z at control point (s, r) to give the coordinates of a point on the Bézier surface. Figure 5.6 shows a series of curves that represent the surface defined by the control points shown in Fig. 5.4.

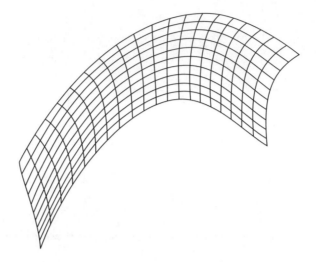

Figure 5.6 Bézier surface defined by control points shown in Fig. 5.4.

A machine has done the hard work of computing and displaying lines join-ing points on the Bézier surface. The result can be rapidly presented to a 3D designer for his reaction, which might be (interactively) to move some of the control points and note the effect that that has on the surface. For example, if the control points that are marked in Fig. 5.4 are all moved by a significant amount then the Bézier surface will look like that shown in Fig. 5.7.

The point to note is that the 3D designer can quickly adjust intermediate control points, and then rapidly see the effect that this 'tweaking' has had on the surface. Eventually, the designer develops a 'feel' for this interaction,

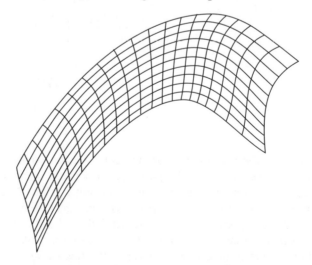

Figure 5.7 Bézier surface 'tweaked' by moving four control points.

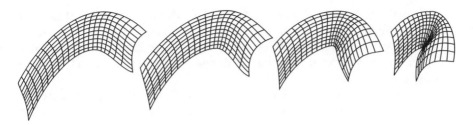

Figure 5.8 Bézier surface rotated so as to provide depth cues.

which is entirely beneficial to the engineering or creative design that is being produced.

The surface can be made to appear more realistic by Gouraud shading or Phong shading, as described in Chapter 11. Either of these shading procedures will give a realistic rendering of the Bézier surface, but at some significant computational expense. Hence, such shading is only considered necessary when the 3D design has been finalised and is to be rendered for sales, or other presentational purposes. During the design process, two sets of orthogonal Bézier curves are normally considered to be a perfectly acceptable rendering, especially as the object can easily be rotated to bring out its three-dimensional characteristics.

Figure 5.8 shows the Bézier surface in four positions. At the left, the rotation around the y axis is the 45° required for an isometric view. The surface has then been rotated through 60°, 90°, and 135° respectively, to produce the other three views. The 3D designer could observe a rotation in real time, and even have the surface oscillating between a range of angular positions. Real time oscillation of a shape rendered in this manner gives the observer (at little computational expense) a very good idea of the geometric characteristics of the 3D object.

5.4 **Summary**

- The users of most computer graphics applications need to be able to draw curves which either pass through every one of a set of control points (interpolation), or pass through the end-points and approximate to the others.
- Parametric cubic curves are widely used because several sections can be concatenated, and both the gradient and the radius of curvature at the transition points are unchanged.
- Bézier curves are a form of cubic curve in which the initial and final gradients are defined by the positions of the intermediate control points.
- The formulation of a Bézier curve is useful, as each term in the summation can be obtained by operations on the previous term.
- Bézier curves are easily extended into three dimensions to create space curves.

- Two orthogonal sets of Bézier space curves define a curved surface. The surface appears as a set of quadrilateral patches or tiles, which can be shaded to yield a realistic image. Alternatively, the surface can be rotated in real time in order to provide the designer with depth cues as ideas are tried out.
- The control points that define a curved surface can be manipulated in such a way as to give the surface some required aesthetic or engineering properties.

5.5 **Further reading**

Almost every book on computer graphics has a great deal to say about parametric cubic curves. Mathematics tends to loom large with this topic and some readers may prefer the more practical approach to be found in the following.

Angel, E., *Interactive Computer Graphics (A Top-Down Approach with OpenGL)*, (2nd edn) Addison Wesley, 1999. An introduction to graphics that emphasises applications programming. Technical implementation issues are discussed.

Bézier, P., *Numerical Control: Mathematics and Applications*, translated by A. R. Forrest and A. F. Pankhurst, John Wiley & Sons, London, 1972.

Foley, J. D., and A. van Dam, *Introduction to Computer Graphics*, Addison Wesley Longman Higher Education, 1993. The presentation is aimed at students, with worked examples in C.

Hill, F. S., *Computer Graphics*, Macmillan Publishing Company, New York, 1990. Textbook covering the concepts and techniques of computer graphics. It aims to teach the writing of programs that produce graphical pictures and images of many kinds of information. Curve and surface design for CAD is well covered.

Exercises

1. Write a simple program using any graphics system to which you have access. The user will specify four control points and the program will compute and display the initial and final gradients of the Bézier curve defined by these points.
2. Adapt the procedure DrawBezierCurve given on page 54, so that the user can specify any number of control points by moving the cursor around the screen, and clicking the mouse button.
3. Enhance your solution to question 2 so that the user may specify the z coordinates of the control points. The program is to display the space curve as seen after it has been rotated 45° around the y axis, followed by 37° around the x axis.

4. The coordinates of the control points illustrated in Fig. 5.4 are as follows (starting at the top set):

X	Y	Z
0.00	2.00	11.00
0.00	4.00	9.00
1.00	8.00	8.00
1.00	10.00	3.00
4.00	13.00	0.00
6.00	11.00	-3.00
7.00	9.00	-4.00
10.00	8.00	-5.00
0.00	-2.00	10.00
0.50	4.00	8.00
1.00	7.00	5.00
2.00	8.00	2.00
4.00	10.00	1.00
6.00	11.00	0.00
7.00	9.00	-1.00
10.00	8.00	-1.00
1.00	-3.00	10.00
1.50	2.00	8.00
2.00	5.00	5.00
2.50	6.00	3.00
4.50	8.00	1.00
7.50	9.00	1.00
9.00	7.00	1.00
12.00	6.00	0.00
1.00	-5.00	10.00
1.50	0.00	8.00
2.00	3.00	5.00
2.50	4.00	3.00
4.50	6.00	1.00
7.50	7.00	1.00
9.00	5.00	1.00
12.00	4.00	0.00

Write a program to plot the control points and join them with lines, as shown in Fig. 5.4. Rotate all the points, using the IsoView procedure given on page 68. Plot space curves through each set of control points. Do they differ from the two orthogonal sets of space curves shown in Fig. 5.6?

5. Why is it important to have continuity of the second derivative at the transition between parametric cubic curves? What other reasons are there for the widespread use of Bézier space curves and surfaces in 3D design?

CHAPTER 6

Three dimensions

6.1 **Introduction**

In Chapter 5, we examined both plane curves and curved surfaces. The latter are, of course, 3-dimensional and served as an introduction to the additional mathematical tools that are required in order to operate in a 3-dimensional environment. We will now look at plane surfaces and see how they relate to that useful 2-dimensional element: the straight line.

6.2 **Homogeneous coordinates**

We have seen how, in 2D, the two constructs that can conveniently be represented by row and column vectors are the *line* and the *point*. In 3D, it is a *plane* and a point that can be represented in homogeneous coordinates. Of course, the extra dimension means that there are four rather than three elements in the vectors.

The 4-element row vector represents a point **P** (in 3D)

$$[u \quad v \quad w \quad q]$$

This maps to cartesian coordinates (x, y, z) as

$$x = u/q, \quad y = v/q \quad \text{and} \quad z = w/q$$

All elements in a row vector may be multiplied by a non-zero constant. Hence

$$[u \quad v \quad w \quad q] = [u/q \quad v/q \quad w/q \quad 1]$$
$$= [x \quad y \quad z \quad 1].$$

In three dimensions, homogeneous coordinates are used to describe an infinite plane as a 4-element column vector which looks like this:

$$\delta = \begin{bmatrix} a \\ b \\ c \\ d \end{bmatrix}$$

A useful way to think of the column vector for a plane is that it specifies the coefficients for the *equation* of the plane. Hence, every point in the plane δ obeys the equation $ax + by + cz + d = 0$.

This is the 3D equivalent of the statement that every point on the line $\begin{bmatrix} a \\ b \\ c \end{bmatrix}$ obeys the equation:

$$ax + by + c = 0$$

A point in 3-space, $\mathbf{P} = [x \quad y \quad z \quad 1]$ lies on the plane $\delta = \begin{bmatrix} a \\ b \\ c \\ d \end{bmatrix}$

if and only if the scalar product $\mathbf{P} \cdot \delta = 0$, i.e. $ax + by + cz + d = 0$.

Like the homogeneous coordinates for a line, the elements in a column vector are parameters with a meaning that can be explained in spatial terms. Suppose that the infinite plane passes through the triangle shown in Fig. 6.1 with vertices at $(X, 0, 0)$, $(0, Y, 0)$, $(0, 0, Z)$.

We then have the three equations

$$aX + 0 \mid 0 + d = 0$$

$$0 + bY + 0 + d = 0$$

$$0 + 0 + cZ + d = 0$$

Whence

$$a = -d/X \quad b = -d/Y \quad c = -d/Z$$

and so the equation of the plane is

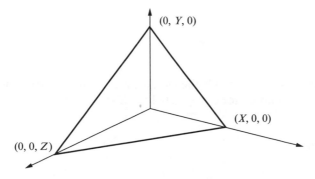

Figure 6.1 Plane defined by three points on axes.

$$-xd/X - yd/Y - zd/Z + d = 0$$

The d terms cancel out to give

$$-x/X - y/Y - z/Z + 1 = 0$$

and hence the plane of the triangle is the following column vector:

$$\delta = \begin{bmatrix} -1/X \\ -1/Y \\ -1/Z \\ 1 \end{bmatrix} = \begin{bmatrix} a \\ b \\ c \\ 1 \end{bmatrix}$$

which shows that if d is made equal to 1 (by dividing all the elements by d) then

$$X = -1/a, \quad Y = -1/b \quad \text{and} \quad Z = -1/c$$

In other words, the coordinates where the plane intersects the three axes can rapidly be computed from the homogeneous coordinates of the plane.

Example 6.1

Where does this plane intersect the axes?

$$\delta = \begin{bmatrix} 2.5 \\ -5.0 \\ 10.0 \\ -12.5 \end{bmatrix}$$

Dividing each of the elements by -12.5 gives

$$a = -1/5, \quad b = 2/5, \quad c = -4/5$$

and hence

$$X = 5.0, \quad Y = -2.5, \quad Z = 1.25$$

~~~

Any plane that passes through the origin of coordinates will have the fourth element of its column vector equal to 0, like this:

$$\delta = \begin{bmatrix} 2.5 \\ -5.0 \\ 10.0 \\ 0.0 \end{bmatrix}$$

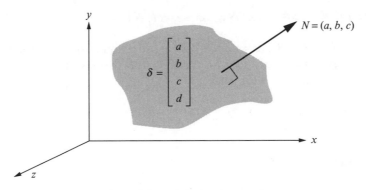

Figure 6.2 Orientation of a plane surface.

Of course, it is *not* permissible to divide all the elements by zero in order to make the fourth element equal to 1. The mere fact that the bottom element is zero proves that the plane passes through the origin.

The orientation of a plane surface in space can be described with the normal vector to the plane, as shown in Fig. 6.2.

This surface normal vector has cartesian coordinates (a, b, c) where a, b, and c are the first three elements in the column vector that describe the plane. So we now have an even more graphical meaning for the homogeneous coordinates. Notice that the fourth element in the column vector apparently plays no part in defining the normal vector. This is because the *length* of the normal vector is arbitrary and $N = (2a, 2b, 2c)$, $N = (a/3, b/3, c/3)$, etc. all specify the same vector *direction*.

However, it is frequently necessary to know the angle that the normal vector makes with each of the positive coordinate axes. Clearly, the length of the normal vector is

$$|N| = \sqrt{a^2 + b^2 + c^2}$$

and hence the angles α, β, γ shown in Fig. 6.3 are given by

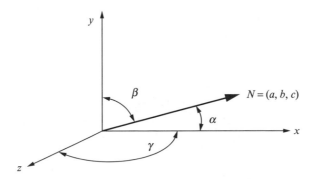

Figure 6.3 Normal vector and direction cosines.

$$\cos \alpha = a/|N|, \quad \cos \beta = b/|N|, \quad \cos \gamma = c/|N|$$

The values $\cos \alpha$, $\cos \beta$, $\cos \gamma$ are called the 'direction cosines' of the vector. It is only necessary to specify two of the direction cosines in order to give the direction of the normal vector since

$$\cos^2 \alpha + \cos^2 \beta + \cos^2 \gamma = 1$$

6.3 **Transformations**

In Chapter 3 we looked at the transformations of translation, scaling and rotation in 2D, and we saw how these transformations may be computed using a 3×3 transformation matrix. In 3D we can use a 4×4 matrix to perform these operations.

For **translation**

$$x' = x + Dx$$

$$y' = y + Dy$$

$$z' = z + Dz$$

Hence

$$\mathbf{P}' = [x + Dx \quad y + Dy \quad z + Dz \quad 1]$$

and the transformation matrix is

$$\begin{bmatrix} 1 & 0 & 0 & 0 \\ 0 & 1 & 0 & 0 \\ 0 & 0 & 1 & 0 \\ Dx & Dy & Dz & 1 \end{bmatrix}$$

For **scaling**

$$x' = xS_x$$

$$y' = yS_y$$

$$z' = zS_z$$

Hence

$$\mathbf{P}' = [xS_x \quad yS_y \quad zS_z \quad 1]$$

and the transformation matrix is

$$\begin{bmatrix} S_x & 0 & 0 & 0 \\ 0 & S_y & 0 & 0 \\ 0 & 0 & S_z & 0 \\ 0 & 0 & 0 & 1 \end{bmatrix}$$

For **rotation** around the z axis, when the point is rotated through angle δ_z

$x' = x \cos \delta_z - y \sin \delta_z$

$y' = x \sin \delta_z + y \cos \delta_z$

$z' = z$

Hence

$$P' = [x \cos \delta_z - y \sin \delta_z \quad x \sin \delta_z + y \cos \delta_z \quad z \quad 1]$$

and the transformation matrix is

$$\begin{bmatrix} \cos \delta_z & \sin \delta_z & 0 & 0 \\ -\sin \delta_z & \cos \delta_z & 0 & 0 \\ 0 & 0 & 1 & 0 \\ 0 & 0 & 0 & 1 \end{bmatrix}$$

For **rotation** around the y axis, when the point is rotated through angle δ_y

$x' = x \cos \delta_y + z \sin \delta_y$

$y' = y$

$z' = -x \sin \delta_y + z \cos \delta_y$

Hence

$$P' = [x \cos \delta_y + z \sin \delta_y \quad y \quad -x \sin \delta_y + z \cos \delta_y \quad 1]$$

and the transformation matrix is

$$\begin{bmatrix} \cos \delta_y & 0 & -\sin \delta_y & 0 \\ 0 & 1 & 0 & 0 \\ \sin \delta_y & 0 & \cos \delta_y & 0 \\ 0 & 0 & 0 & 1 \end{bmatrix}$$

For **rotation** around the x axis, when the point is rotated through angle δ_x

$x' = x$

$y' = y \cos \delta_x - z \sin \delta_x$

$z' = y \sin \delta_x + z \cos \delta_x$

Hence

$$\mathbf{P}' = [x \quad y \cos \delta_x - z \sin \delta_x \quad y \sin \delta_x + z \cos \delta_x \quad 1]$$

and the transformation matrix is

$$\begin{bmatrix} 1 & 0 & 0 & 0 \\ 0 & \cos \delta_x & \sin \delta_x & 0 \\ 0 & -\sin \delta_x & \cos \delta_x & 0 \\ 0 & 0 & 0 & 1 \end{bmatrix}$$

Unlike the other transformations, the order in which rotations are carried out is significant. In other words, a rotation of 45° around the z axis, followed by a rotation of −30° around the y axis will give entirely different transformed coordinates compared with a rotation of −30° around the y axis, followed by a rotation of 45° around the z axis. (There is an exercise at the end of this chapter where you can demonstrate this for yourself.) Therefore, it is essential

```
void IsoView (float x, float y, float z,
              float & xt, float & yt, float & zt)

{
const float cos45 = 1.0 / sqrt(2.0);
const float sin45 = -cos45;
const float cosiso = sqrt(2.0) / sqrt(3.0);
const float siniso = 1.0 / sqrt(3.0);

float x1, y1, z1;

x1 = z * sin45 + x * cos45;
y1 = y;
z1 = z * cos45 - x * sin45;

xt = x1;
yt = y1 * cosiso - z1 * siniso;
zt = y1 * siniso + z1 * cosiso;
}
```

Figure 6.4 Rotation transformation for an isometric view.

when specifying rotations around axes to have a convention for the order in which they are carried out. For the right-hand system shown in Fig. 1.4 (page 5), the rotations are carried out first around the z axis, then around the y axis, and finally around the x axis.

One very useful series of rotations of this kind can be used to create an 'isometric' view of a solid object. Figure 5.3 on page 55 is such an isometric view. Notice that the x axis is inclined at $-30°$ to the horizontal, and that the z axis is inclined at $-150°$. This effect is produced by rotating a solid object through $-45°$ around the y axis and then rotating it through $\tan^{-1}(1/\sqrt{2})$ around the x axis. C++ code for carrying out this simple but useful transformation is given in Fig. 6.4.

6.4 Polygonal plane surfaces

When modelling solid objects, we are dealing with polygonal surfaces that enclose (or bound) the interior of an object. It is vital to be able to distinguish between the two sides of the surface. If the edges of each polygon are specified in the conventional 'INSIDE is to the *left* of a vector' direction when viewing the outer side of th plane, then the direction of the normal vector will be from inside to outside.

In Chapter 5 we looked to two orthogonal sets of Bézier space curves and noted that the 'patches' or 'tiles' on the resulting Bézier curved surface are approximately plane quadrilaterals. Hence, the coordinates of four points lying in (approximately) the same plane are known. In theory, we could select any three of the four points, set up three simultaneous plane equations, and solve for the homogeneous coordinates of a specific 'patch'. In practice, a random selection of points in a plane is unsuitable, because there is always the possibility that they lie on the same straight line, and hence do not define a plane. A practicable solution is to use all the coordinates of *all* the points that may be considered to lie in the same plane, and the equation given on page 70 can then be used to compute the 'best fit' plane for a small part of the curved surface.

This solution was devised by Martin Newell and popularised by Newman and Sproull in the book recommended at the end of this chapter.

If the three points chosen are definitely *not* collinear and their coordinates are

$$(x_0, y_0, z_0), \quad (x_1, y_1, z_1), \quad (x_2, y_2, z_2)$$

then it may be shown that

$$a = y_0(z_1 - z_2) + y_1(z_2 - z_0) + y_2(z_0 - z_1)$$
$$b = z_0(x_1 - x_2) + z_1(x_2 - x_0) + z_2(x_0 - x_1)$$
$$c = x_0(y_1 - y_2) + x_1(y_2 - y_0) + x_2(y_0 - y_1)$$

and d is found by back substitution:

$$d = -x_0(y_1z_2 - y_2z_1) - x_1(y_2z_0 - y_0z_2) - x_2(y_0z_1 - y_1z_0).$$

If (as is frequently the case) more than three points lie in the same plane, then it is possible to avoid the need to check for linearity of three randomly chosen points by generalising the above equations. If there are n points then the Newell equations are:

$$a = \sum_{r=0}^{n-1}(y_r - y_s)(z_r + z_s) \quad \text{where } s = (r+1) \bmod n$$

$$b = \sum_{r=0}^{n-1}(z_r - z_s)(x_r + x_s)$$

$$c = \sum_{r=0}^{n-1}(x_r - x_s)(y_r + y_s)$$

N.B. $(r + 1)$ **mod** n means 'the remainder when $(r + 1)$ is divided by n'. Hence, when $r + 1 = n$ the remainder is zero and the coordinate of the first vertex goes into the summation.

Example 6.2

The following points all lie in the same plane. Compute the normal vector to the plane, and the angle between this normal and the x and y axes. Determine where the plane intersects the three axes.

x	y	z
2.5	5.0	0.3
7.5	10.0	-0.7
-5.0	0.0	2.8
-10.0	2.5	6.8
0.0	7.5	2.8

Using the above equations

$$a = 2.00 + 21.00 - 24.00 - 48.00 + 7.75 = -41.25$$

$$b = 10.00 - 8.75 + 60.00 - 40.00 + 6.25 = 27.50$$

$$c = -75.00 + 125.00 + 12.50 - 100.00 - 31.25 = -68.75$$

$$d = -ax_0 - by_0 - cz_0 = -13.75$$

Therefore the plane is

$$\delta = \begin{bmatrix} -41.25 \\ 27.50 \\ -68.75 \\ -13.75 \end{bmatrix} = \begin{bmatrix} 3 \\ -2 \\ 5 \\ 1 \end{bmatrix}$$

and its normal vector is $N = (3, -2, 5)$.

The length of this normal is given by

$$|N| = \sqrt{a^2 + b^2 + c^2} = \sqrt{9 + 4 + 25} = \sqrt{38}$$

hence

$$\cos \alpha = 3/\sqrt{38}, \quad \cos \beta = -2/\sqrt{38}$$

and as it is more practicable to find the inverse of the tangent:

$$\tan \alpha = \sqrt{29}/3, \quad \tan \beta = \sqrt{34}/(-2)$$

to give

$$\alpha = 60.878° \quad \beta = 108.932°$$

It was shown on page 00 that the intercepts on the three axes are given by

$$X = -1/a, \quad Y = -1/b \quad \text{and} \quad Z = -1/c$$

hence

$$X = -1/3, \quad Y = 1/2 \quad \text{and} \quad Z = -1/5$$

6.5 Intersecting planes

If there are two non-parallel planes

$$a_1 x + b_1 y + c_1 z + 1 = 0 \quad \text{and} \quad a_2 x + b_2 y + c_2 z + 1 = 0$$

then they will intersect and the intersection line can be found by solving the equations simultaneously. This gives

$$(a_1 - a_2)x + (b_1 - b_2)y + (c_1 - c_2)z = 0$$

If the first plane is a polygonal surface that bounds a solid object, and the second plane is a horizontal plane with equation $y = Y$, then $a_2 = 0$, $b_2 = -1/Y$ and $c_2 = 0$.

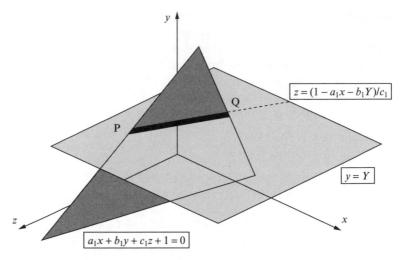

Figure 6.5 Horizontal plane intersecting triangular surface.

Hence it will intersect the first plane to create a line in the xz plane with equation

$$z = (1 - a_1x - b_1 Y)/c_1$$

as shown in Fig. 6.5.

The concept of cutting a bounding polygon with a horizontal plane and computing the equation of the resulting straight line in the xz plane is thoroughly exploited by the so-called 'scan line' algorithm. The scan line algorithm renders a solid object correctly by slicing through the object at the y value of each scan line of the display and computing the resulting cross-section.

This sectioning technique is the mathematical equivalent of the mechanical process that was carried out in order to produce the cross-sections of the 'Visual Man' referred to in Chapter 2. Once the cross-section has been computed, it is possible to determine which surfaces are hidden by those closer to the viewer, and hence to render only the surface that is visible along a particular scan line.

The process of computing the cross-section at a scan plane is not a trivial one, as it is necessary to determine where the intersection line begins and ends. In other words, the (x, z) coordinates of points $\mathbf{P}$ and $\mathbf{Q}$ in Fig. 6.5 must be computed. This may be done by finding the plane which 'owns' the edges for which valid intersections have been computed. Details of this process are given in Chapter 9.

6.6 Summary

- In 3D we use a four-element row vector to represent a point, and a four-element column vector to represent a plane. A point lies in a plane if the scalar product of the two vectors is zero.

- Its normal vector conveniently describes the orientation of a plane surface in space. The vector starts at the origin, and the coordinates of its finish point are the first three elements of the plane's column vector.
- The cosines of the angles between the normal vector and the three axes are dubbed the *direction cosines* of the plane. They are a very convenient way of determining if a viewer can see anything of the outside of a plane.
- In many computer graphics applications, the user interactively specifies (via the Graphical User Interface) a number of points that lie in the same plane. The homogeneous coordinates of such a plane are readily computed using the Newell equations.
- Two non-parallel planes will intersect to give a straight line. Solving the two plane equations simultaneously derives the equation of such a line. Hence, it is possible to determine precisely where the intersection line starts and finishes on a finite plane surface, such as one bounding a solid object.

6.7 **Further reading**

For greater detail of the application of some of the mathematics presented in this chapter, the following are recommended.

Gasson, P. C., *Geometry of Spatial Forms*, Ellis Horwood, Chichester, 1983. Lots of useful geometry. Homogeneous coordinates normal vectors and direction cosines are well explained.

Firebaugh, M. W., *Computer Graphics. Tools for Visualization*, Wm. C. Brown Publishers, Dubuque, 1993. Highly practical approach. Focused on Macintosh applications, but easy to transport algorithms to the PC.

Newman, W. M. and R. F. Sproull, *Principles of Interactive Computer Graphics*, McGraw-Hill, New York, 1979. The classic book, which first brought the robust Newell equations to the attention of a wider readership.

Exercises

1. Which of these points

$P = [-3.60 \quad 2.90 \quad 7.21 \quad 16.20]$, $\quad Q = [0.22 \quad -0.18 \quad -0.46 \quad -1.00]$,
$R = [-0.22 \quad 0.18 \quad 0.44 \quad 1.00]$, $\quad S = [-18.00 \quad 14.50 \quad 36.00 \quad 81.00]$

lie in the plane $\delta = \begin{bmatrix} 3.50 \\ -2.70 \\ 9.80 \\ -3.10 \end{bmatrix}$?

2. Where does the plane $\delta = \begin{bmatrix} 0.5 \\ -2.6 \\ 7.8 \\ -4.1 \end{bmatrix}$ intersect the three axes?

3. The normal vector to a plane is at an angle of 30° to the x axis and 60° to the y axis. What are the homogeneous coordinates of the plane?

4.   A cube of side 1.0 with its centroid at the origin will have vertices at:

(−0.5, −0.5, 0.5), (0.5, −0.5, 0.5), (0.5, 0.5, 0.5), (−0.5, 0.5, 0.5),
(−0.5, −0.5, −0.5), (0.5, −0.5, −0.5), (0.5, 0.5, −0.5), (−0.5, 0.5, −0.5)

Compute the transformed coordinates

a) when the cube is rotated through 30° around the z axis, followed by a rotation of −60° around the y axis,

b) when the cube is rotated −60° around the y axis, followed by a rotation of 30° around the z axis (not the conventional order).

Plot the transformed coordinates on grid paper and sketch the rotated cubes. Are there any significant differences between them?

Use the correct angles of rotation to transform the cube into an isometric view. Plot the result on grid paper. What is the apparent length of a side of the cube now?

5. The following six vertices all lie in the same plane:

(−0.22, 0.18, 0.44), (0.11, 0.12, 0.31), (0.59, 0.49, 0.24),
(0.21, 0.15, 0.28), (0.21, 0.02, 0.25), (0.23, 0.20, 0.29).

Find the homogeneous coordinates of the plane using:

• a pocket calculator
• a spreadsheet
• a simple program that you have written in which the six sets of coordinates are stored in a suitable constant array.

6. In question 5, the smallest value of y is 0.02, and the largest is 0.49. Write down the equations of the lines where the horizontal planes

$$y = 0.02 \quad \text{and} \quad y = 0.49$$

intersect the inclined plane.
What are the values of x and z at these y values?

CHAPTER 7

Modelling natural objects

7.1 **Introduction**

In Chapters 5 and 6, we considered object representations that use Euclidean geometry methods. In other words, *equations* (such as those for a plane or a space curve) were used to describe components that could be assembled in order to model a solid object. Such methods are suitable for describing manufactured objects that have smooth surfaces and regular shapes. Natural objects, like coastlines, mountains and rivers, have highly irregular features. So do most living things: trees, plants, cells, bones – all have very complex boundaries.

Clearly, Euclidean methods are unsuitable for describing such natural shapes. The number of equations required to describe the coastline of a small island would easily exceed 10^3, and the surface of a minor mountain would need of the order of 10^6 equations to define it accurately. However, natural objects can be readily described using fractal geometry methods. Instead of equations, *procedures* are used to model a single natural object, or an entire landscape.

Apart from the obvious problems of processing a large number of equations, the objection to using equations to describe natural objects is that storage space is wasted. What is generally required by the computer graphics user is to zoom into an object in order to see more detail. With equations, that detail must always be present in memory and most of it does not appear on the display screen. On the other hand, a procedure can render as little or as much detail as required. For example, the coastline of the Isle of Wight, as seen from a satellite, can be rendered with no more then ten straight lines. Zooming in, more and shorter lines can be added procedurally to give detail that is appropriate for the scale.

Practically all of the procedures that have been published for rendering natural objects make use of fractal geometry. The full mathematics of fractals is outside the scope of this book, so most of the following examples put the emphasis on the application of certain classes of fractals in computer graphics.

7.2 **What is a fractal?**

A fractal object has two basic characteristics:

- infinite detail at every point,
- a self-similarity between the object parts and the overall features of the object.

If we zoom into a Euclidean shape, eventually the view will become smooth and almost featureless. Zooming into a fractal object yields just as much detail as in the original shape. A mountain modelled as a fractal object will continue to have the same jagged shape even when only a tiny part of the mountain remains in the viewing window. This is because any view of a fractal object uses the same procedures to generate the picture, no matter how small a part of the total object is visible.

We describe the amount of variation in the object detail with a number called the 'fractal dimension'. Unlike the Euclidean dimension (where we refer to two or three dimensions), the fractal dimension is not necessarily an integer. The basis of the word 'fractal' comes from the fact that such objects were originally described as having a 'fractional dimension'.

A fractal object is generated by repeatedly applying a specified transformation function to points within a region of space. If $P_0 = (x_0, y_0, z_0)$ is a selected initial point, each iteration of a transformation function F generates successive levels of detail with the equations

$$P_1 = F(P_0), \quad P_2 = F(P_1), \quad P_3 = F(P_2), \ldots$$

The transformation function can be applied to

- a specified set of points,
- an initial set of primitives, such as straight lines, curves, surfaces, or solid objects.

Either deterministic or random generation procedures can be used at each iteration. The transformation function may be defined in terms of

- geometric transformations, such as translation, scaling, rotation,
- non-linear coordinate transformations and decision parameters.

By definition, fractal objects contain infinite detail. However, in practice the transformation function is applied a finite number of times and therefore the objects displayed by this method have finite dimensions. When a fractal object is rendered to a graphics display, the amount of detail depends upon the number of iterations performed and on the resolution of the display system. To see the object in more detail it is necessary to zoom in on a selected part of the display and repeat the transformation function iterations.

7.3 **A simple example**

The snowflake is an ideal example of a natural object that can be modelled by starting with a set of primitives, then transforming them with the transformations of scaling and rotation. This example is classified as a **deterministic** (non-random) **self-similar** fractal. The starting shape is called the 'inititator'. Subparts of the initiator are then replaced with a pattern, called the 'generator'. Figure 7.1 shows the initiator (left) and generator (right) of the **Koch** curve.

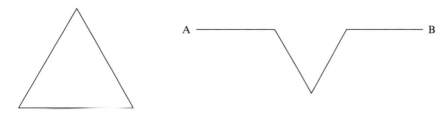

Figure 7.1 Initiator and generator of the Koch curve.

Each of the three sides of the initiator is replaced by a transformation of the generator. Firstly, the generator is scaled so that the distance AB is equal to the length of the line that is being replaced. Secondly, the scaled generator is rotated so that direction AB is the same as that of the line that is being replaced. The result of this first iteration will be the 6-pointed star pattern shown in Fig. 7.2.

Figure 7.2 One iteration of the transformation.

There are twelve sides in Fig. 7.2, and if each is replaced by the scaled-down generator then we start to get a rudimentary snowflake, as shown in Fig. 7.3.

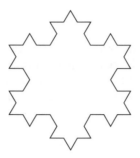

Figure 7.3 Shape resulting from two iterations.

The length of each line segment in the initiator increases by a factor of 4/3 at each iteration. The length of the fractal tends to infinity as more detail is added. After four iterations, the snowflake has 768 segments, as in Fig. 7.4.

Figure 7.4 Shape resulting from four iterations.

If you look carefully at the deliberately enlarged snowflake in Fig. 7.4, you can distinguish each line segment. However, the object of the exercise is to model natural objects, and there is no point in rendering detail that cannot be distinguished by the human eye. The great advantage of the procedural method is that only the necessary amount of detail need be shown. Once a line segment is only a single pixel, then clearly there is no need of further iterations. If the user wishes to zoom in on a small part of the object, then it is only necessary to process that part of the object that will appear in the viewport.

This first example of fractal geometry has been chosen for its simplicity of implementation, and Fig. 7.4 demonstrates that the technique can indeed convincingly render this type of natural object. However, a snow crystal is a special case with many axes of symmetry and nothing random in its make up. Most natural objects do not have such symmetry, and they do exhibit random features. It is to such objects that we now turn our attention.

7.4 **Fractal classification**

One property that neatly distinguishes two distinct classes of fractals is the role of chance played in their generation and resulting structure. We therefore have the following dichotomy.

- deterministic fractals,
- stochastic fractals.

Deterministic fractals have structures that are fixed uniquely by the algorithm employed in their creation. In other words, for a given set of parameters, a deterministic fractal generator will produce identical structures each time it is run. Chance plays no role in the final structure of the deterministic fractal.

Stochastic fractals are characterised by the fact that random processes play a central role in determining the structure of the fractal object. Phenomena such as turbulence, seacoast, and mountain formation are deterministic at a physical level, but are extremely sensitive to the *initial* conditions. Such extreme sensitivity is a property of all chaotic systems. It is impracticable to write algorithms that attempt to simulate the correct initial conditions, and so random processes (e.g. a random number generator) are used in the generation of the graphics.

Another way to classify fractals is by looking at the nature of the algorithms by which they are generated. There are four distinct classes:

- linear replacement mapping,
- iterated function systems,
- complex plane mapping,
- stochastic processes.

Linear replacement mapping works on the principle that a generator function maps a given structure onto a new more complex one, as we have seen for the Koch curve.

Iterated function systems generate fractals by the successive application of a series of contractive affine transformations.

Complex plane mapping facilitates the generation of mathematical objects such as the Julia and Mandelbrot sets. They are generated by successive mapping on the complex plane.

Stochastic processes employ random processes with a recursive algorithm. There is also a mathematical classification of fractals into three types:

- self-similar,
- self-affine,
- invariant set.

Self-similar fractals have parts, each of which is a scaled down version of the entire object, or (like the snowflake above) is a scaled down generator. Starting from an initial shape, the object subparts are constructed by applying a scaling parameter s to the overall shape. We can use the same scaling factor for all subparts, or we can use different scaling factors for different scaled down parts of the object. If we also apply random variations to the scaled down sub-parts, the fractal is said to be 'statistically self-similar'. Statistically self-similar fractals are commonly used to model

- trees,
- shrubs,
- certain plants.

Self-affine fractals have parts that are formed with different scaling parameters s_x, s_y, and s_z along the three axes. If we also apply random variations to the scaled down sub-parts, the fractal is said to be 'statistically self-affine'. Statistically self-affine fractals are commonly used to model

- terrain,
- water,
- clouds.

Invariant fractal sets are formed with non-linear transformations. This class of fractals includes self-squaring fractals, such as the Mandelbrot Set (see page 90), which are formed with squaring functions in complex space. It also includes self-inverse fractals, formed with inversion procedures.

7.5 **Fractal construction**

Self-similar fractal construction of a *surface* may be illustrated by making from card the following model. The base of the model is a regular tetrahedron with equilateral triangular surfaces, each side of which is 20 cm in length. Tape the edges together to create the 3D shape. Next, you are going to add a smaller tetrahedron to each surface of the original. You need sixteen equilateral triangles of side 10 cm. When you have taped them together to make four tetrahedra, fix them centrally on each of the original four surfaces of the tetrahedron, so that vertices are at the mid points of the original. Each face of the original tetrahedron is converted to six smaller faces and the face area is increased by a factor of 3/2. The resulting model should look like Fig. 7.5.

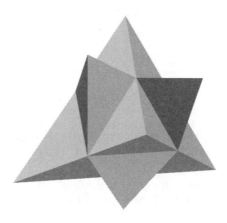

Figure 7.5 Self-similar surface construction.

Another way to create self-similar fractal objects is to punch holes in a given initiator. This is similar to the 2D **difference** operation described in Chapter 4, whereas adding more surface area is like the **union** operation.

There are two practicable ways to introduce randomness into the construction of a self-similar fractal:

- choose a generator randomly at each step from a set of predefined shapes,
- compute coordinate displacements randomly.

A natural-looking outline can be created by selecting a random, midpoint displacement distance at each step. Figure 7.6 shows the same initiator as Fig. 7.1.

There are three iterations produced by randomly displacing the midpoint of each of the lines in the previous iteration. In each iteration, the thin dashed lines indicate the 'parent' of the two new edges.

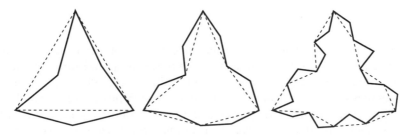

Figure 7.6 Three iterations generated by random midpoint displacement.

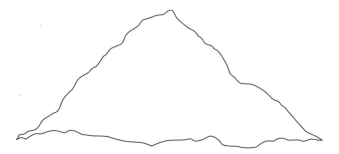

Figure 7.7 Six or more iterations produce natural-looking objects.

In order to produce the appearance of a natural object, a large number of iterations is required, but that is the great advantage of computer-generated graphics: the computer does the hard work. Figure 7.7 has a passable resemblance to the profile of a mountain and its foothills. It required six iterations to generate 192 short straight lines from the original three.

7.5.1 *Affine Fractal-Construction Methods*

We can obtain highly realistic representations for terrain and other natural objects using affine fractal methods that model object features as **fractional Brownian motion**. This is an extension of standard Brownian motion, a form of 'random walk' that describes the erratic zigzag movement of particles in a gas or other fluid. Figure 7.8 illustrates a random walk path in the xy plane.

Figure 7.8 Model of fractional Brownian motion.

Starting from a given position, we generate a straight-line segment in a random direction and with a random length. We then move to the end-point of the first line segment and repeat the process. This procedure is repeated for any number of line segments, and we calculate the statistical properties of the line path over any time interval t. **Fractional Brownian motion** is obtained by adding an additional parameter to the statistical distribution describing Brownian motion. This additional parameter sets the fractal dimension for the 'motion' path.

A single fractional Brownian path can be used to model a fractal *curve*. With a 2-dimensional array of random fractional Brownian elevations over a ground plane grid, we can model the *surface* of a mountain by connecting the elevations to form a set of polygon patches. If random elevations are generated on the surface of a sphere, we can model the mountains, valleys, and oceans of a planet.

7.6 Self-squaring fractals

Some of the earliest work in what Mandelbrot later named 'fractal geometry' was done by the French mathematicians, Gaston Julia (1883–1978) and Pierre Fatou (1878–1929). They studied the effects of iterative mapping of points on the complex plane. Ultimately, Mandelbrot recognised the unifying principles and 'invented' fractal geometry. The Julia and Mandelbrot sets are two of the most beautiful and interesting complex mathematical objects yet discovered. Each set was originally investigated using iterations of the complex mapping

$$z_{n+1} = z_n^2 + \lambda$$

where z_{n+1}, z_n and λ are all complex numbers.

In two dimensions, a complex number can be represented as $z = x + iy$, where x and y are real numbers, and $i^2 = -1$. x is the real part and y is the imaginary part. It is convenient to think of them as the x coordinate and the y coordinate and map them in 2D as such.

Polar coordinates provide an alternative useful form for complex numbers. Referring to Fig. 2.3 on page 12, we see that the relationship between cartesian and polar coordinates is

$$x = r \cos \theta \quad y = r \sin \theta$$

where

$$r = \sqrt{x^2 + y^2} \quad \text{and} \quad \theta = \tan^{-1}(y/x)$$

Hence, a complex number,

$$z = r(\cos \theta + i \sin \theta)$$

It may be shown that $\cos \theta + i \sin \theta = e^{i\theta}$ (e is the base of natural logarithms) and so a complex number z can be written as

$$z = re^{i\theta}$$

r is termed the **modulus** of the complex number and θ is its **phase**. The polar representation simplifies the computation of functions of complex numbers.

For example, the square root of z is a new complex number z' and the two numbers are simply related by the equation

$$z' = re^{i\theta/2}$$

from which it is obvious that z and z' have the same *modulus*, but the *phase* of z' is half that of z.

We now introduce a useful concept identified by John Guckenheimer in the field of **catastrophe theory**. Guckenheimer (and others) have identified new mathematical structures they call 'strange attractors'. Julia sets can be explained by combining the concept of strange attractors with iterative mapping on the complex plane. The Julia set of the polynomial mapping function, $F(z)$, is the boundary between the basin of attraction of the strange attractor at $z = 0$ and a strange attractor at $z = \infty$.

First consider a case of the simple quadratic function: $F(z) = z'$.

This is a special case of $z_{n+1} = z_n^2 + \lambda$ for which $\lambda = 0$. When mapped onto the xy plane, all points on the z plane fall into one of the following three categories:

- points with modulus > 1, which flee to the attractor at ∞,
- points with modulus < 1, which spiral into the attractor at $(0, 0)$,
- points with modulus = 1 define the chaotic Julia set on the unit circle.

The first two cases are illustrated in Fig. 7.9.

When modulus = 1, the function always maps exactly onto the circumference of the circle. Depending upon the starting point, and the number of iterations, there will be many different points on the circumference of the unit circle. Figure 7.10 was drawn by a computer program that was instructed to place a small circle at each of the 1000 transformed points. As you can see, every one

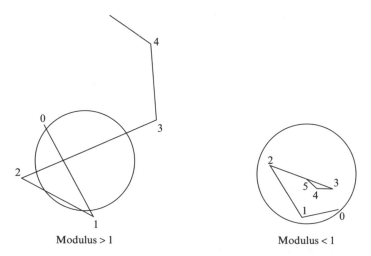

Figure 7.9 The effect of strange attractors.

Figure 7.10 Chaotic Julia set on the unit circle.

lies on the unit circle. Although all the points have the same modulus, they do not have the same *phase*, but many of the points do have exactly the same phase as ones that were drawn earlier. This is why there appears to be so much less then one thousand points.

The addition of a single, complex constant to the transformation produces a family of Julia sets, most of which are interesting, and some of which an abstract artist would have been proud to create. These intriguing quadratic Julia sets arise for various choices of λ in the transformation:

$$F(z) = z^2 + \lambda$$

There are three algorithms for plotting the Julia sets corresponding to the boundaries of the strange attractor basins at (0, 0) and ∞. We can classify these as follows:

- backward mapping,
- forward mapping,
- boundary scanning.

Backward mapping is suggested by an examination of Fig. 7.9 when modulus > 1. Notice that each successive point is further from the unit circle boundary than the preceding one. This suggests that, if the mapping direction is reversed, the Julia set itself will act as an attractor, and in fact that is exactly what happens.

Since the forward iteration is defined as $z_{n+1} = z_n^2 + \lambda$, we can reverse the direction of motion by writing the equation as $z_n = z_{n+1}^2 + \lambda$. Hence:

$$z_{n+1} = \pm\sqrt{z_n - \lambda}$$

There are two roots for each iteration of the backward mapping algorithm, and one may be chosen at random. The fatal flaw with this algorithm is that, having been attracted to the Julia set, succeeding points tend to depart from it and spiral into the strange attractor at (0, 0). Backward mapping is not regarded as a practicable algorithm.

The forward mapping algorithm iterates on each point in the vicinity of the Julia set to see if it flees to (0, 0) or ∞ or lies on the Julia set. This algorithm is ideally suited for pixel-mapped graphics. The technique is to examine each of

```
void FilledJulia(void)

{
   struct Complex {
     float r, i;
   };

   const float scale = 0.01;
   const float R = 10;
   const int Niterations = 100;

   int n, row, col;
   bool Done100, FlownOff;
   Complex z, znew, c;

   c.r = -0.4; // Settings for
   c.i = -0.6; // Fig 7.14

   Canvas->Pen->Width = 1;         // set pen width to 1 pixel
   Canvas->Pen->Style = psSolid;  // set pen style to solid
   Canvas->Pen->Color = clBlue;   // set pen colour to blue

   for ( col = 1; col < 400; col++ )
     {

     for ( row = 1; row < 400; row++ )
       {
       z.r = ( col - 200 ) * scale;
       z.i = ( row - 200 ) * scale;
       Done100 = false;
       FlownOff = false;
       n = 0;

       while ( Done100 + FlownOff == false )
         // Iterations not complete and not yet attracted
         {
         n++;
         znew.r = z.r * z.r - z.i * z.i; // Complex multiplication
         znew.i = z.r * z.i + z.i * z.r; // Complex addition
         z.r = znew.r + c.r;
         z.i = znew.i + c.i;
         if ( z.r*z.r + z.i*z.i > R ) FlownOff = true;
         if ( n > Niterations ) Done100 = true;
         }
       if (Done100) Canvas->Ellipse(col-1, row-1, col+1, row+1);
         // draw a circle one pixel in radius, centre at (col, row)
       }

   }
}
```

Figure 7.11 Function to compute and plot a Julia set.

the pixels in the viewport and test if it is attracted to *i*. If it is not, then the pixel is set. The result has been dubbed a 'filled-in' Julia set, because, of course, it includes both pixels on the boundary *and* those inside it. Nevertheless, the results are pleasing and can often be used to model natural objects, which is the principal objective. A C++ implementation of the forward mapping algorithm is given in Fig. 7.11.

Notice that there are two loops that increment through 400 rows and 400 columns of pixels. The coordinates of a point are computed by applying a suitable scaling factor to the row and to the column number. A point is plotted if it has *not* flown to either zero or infinity after 100 iterations. A point is rendered by drawing a circle that is 2 pixels in diameter. For clarity, the multiplication and the addition of complex numbers is carried out directly within the central `while` loop.

Some sample outputs from the program listed in Fig. 7.11 are reproduced below. The first was produced from ten iterations with $\lambda = (0, 1)$.

Notice the skewed symmetry of Fig. 7.12. Just using one half of the filled-in set facilitates the modelling of natural objects such as branches, river tributaries, and cracks. In general, it will be necessary to select part of any self-squaring fractal, and to 'tweak' the value of λ a little in order to model a particular natural object.

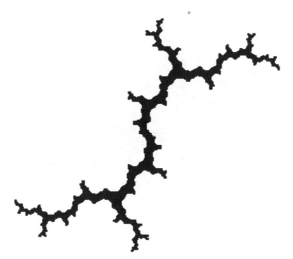

Figure 7.12 Filled-in Julia set from 10 iterations with $\lambda = (0, 1)$.

The second example (Fig. 7.13) was produced from twenty iterations with $\lambda = (-0.4, -0.6)$. This does not lend itself to modelling a natural object, but such sets can be useful in computer graphics, as the procedural method is much the most efficient way of storing and rendering a complex shape.

Figure 7.13 Filled-in Julia set from 20 iterations with $\lambda = (-0.4, -0.6)$.

Figure 7.14 has exactly the same value of λ as Fig. 7.13. The only difference is the number of iterations. Why should the final fractal shape depend upon the number of iterations?

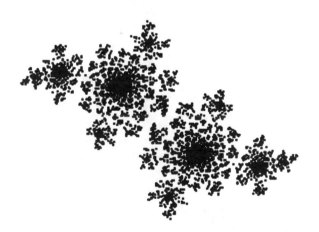

Figure 7.14 Filled-in Julia set from 100 iterations with $\lambda = (-0.4, -0.6)$.

This phenomenon was once dismissed as a mere side effect due to rounding errors when real numbers are not stored accurately. However, if the program is modified to use higher-precision arithmetic then the results are identical. The conclusion must be that the effect is real and the true Julia set is a disconnected set of points, rather than the connected one shown in Fig. 7.13.

A boundary scanning algorithm combines the forward mapping algorithm with the formal definition of Julia sets as the boundary between the two basins of attraction. A pixel is set if it does not flee to an attractor, but an adjacent pixel does. This algorithm, like 'backward mapping', displays the true Julia set. It is often said to be computationally expensive, and is not a practicable way to render natural-looking objects.

```
void Mandelbrot(void)
{
struct Complex {
        float r, i;
      };

int i, j, k, n, row, col, Niter, hue, done, gone, dec, sign;
float x, y, scale, R;
Complex z, znew, c;

scale = 0.005;
R = 10.0;
Niter = 1000;
n = 0;

for (col = 1; col < 400; col++)
  {
  for (row = 1; row < 200; row++)
    {
    z.r = 0.0;
    z.i = 0.0;
    c.r = (col - 100)*scale;
    c.i = (200 - row)*scale;
    done = 0;
    gone = 0;
    n = 0;
    while (done + gone == 0)
      {
      n = n + 1;
      znew.r = z.r * z.r - z.i * z.i;
      znew.i = z.r * z.i + z.i * z.r;
      z.r = znew.r - c.r;
      z.i = znew.i - c.i;
      if (z.r*z.r + z.i*z.i > R) gone = 1;
      if (n > Niter) done = 1;
      }

      // Select a colour according to the number of iterations
      // Plot the point as a circle of 2 pixels diameter
      Canvas->Ellipse(col - 1, row - 1, col + 1, row + 1);
      Canvas->Ellipse(col - 1, 399 - row, col + 1, 401 - row);

    } // end of row for loop
  } // end of column for loop
}
```

Figure 7.15 Procedure to compute and plot the Mandelbrot set.

A very famous fractal shape is obtained from the Mandelbrot Set. It is generated on the complex plane as the set of points (μ_r, μ_i) which, when successively mapped with the function,

$$z_{n+1} = z_n^2 - \mu$$

do not cause the complex number z_n to fly off to infinity.

The above transformation is implemented by first choosing a window in the complex plane. Positions in this window are then mapped to colour-coded pixel positions in a selected screen viewport. The pixel colours are chosen according to the rate of divergence of the corresponding point in the complex plane under the above transformation. In simple (if not entirely accurate) terms, it is like colouring in the space between adjacent contours on a map according to how close together the contours are.

An algorithm can be written by making a minor modification to the forward mapping code used for Julia sets. The fascination inspired by the Mandelbrot

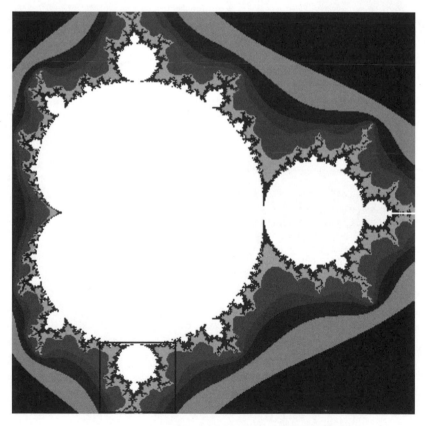

Figure 7.16 The Mandelbrot set with 100 iterations.

set stems from several sources. This set exhibits all of the features discussed above; in particular it has an infinite complexity that emerges as it is explored in finer and finer detail. Hence, it has been used to generate all sorts of special effects for films and television. It also provides some fascinating animations that run on modern personal computers.

Like all fractals, the further you zoom into the Mandelbrot Set, the more detail is revealed. The area near lower left, marked with a rectangle in Fig. 7.16, looks moderately complex at that level of detail. Contrast it with Fig. 7.17, and this important characteristic of fractal geometry is immediately obvious. Creative artists have 'explored' the Mandelbrot Set thoroughly in search of stimulating, abstract shapes, and it is still yielding a rich harvest.

Figure 7.17 Zoom into the area marked on Fig. 7.16.

7.7 **Summary**

- Fractals provide a highly practicable method of modelling natural objects.
- The amount of variation in the object detail is described with a number called the 'fractal dimension', which is not necessarily an integer.
- The word 'fractal' comes from 'fractional dimension'.
- If chance plays *no* part in the generation of a fractal then it is said to be 'deterministic'. Otherwise, the fractal is described as 'stochastic'.
- Fractals can be classified according to the nature of the algorithm that generates them:

  - linear replacement mapping,
  - iterated function systems,
  - complex plane mapping,
  - stochastic processes.

  Alternatively, they can be classified mathematically:

  - self-similar,
  - self-affine,
  - invariant set.

- Deterministic fractals are useful for natural objects, such as crystals and droplets that have axes of symmetry. Stochastic processes are better for natural, rugged objects whose shape has been determined by random events, such as the weather.
- Self-squaring fractals such as the Julia and Mandelbrot set generate a vast range of complex shapes. The Julia set tends to produce some natural-looking objects, such as cracks. The Mandelbrot set is often exploited for the generation of abstract, decorative effects.

7.8 **Further reading**

For greater detail of the application of some of the mathematics presented in this chapter, the following are recommended.

Barnsley, M. F., *Fractals Everywhere*, Academic Press Inc., Boston, 1988.

Firebaugh, M. W., *Computer Graphics – Tools for Visualization*, Wm. C. Brown Publishers, Dubuque, 1993.

Mandelbrodt B. B., *The Fractal Geometry of Nature*, W. H. Freeman & Company, New York, 1983.

Pruskinkiewicz, P., A. Lindenmayer, and J. Hanan, 'Developmental Models of Herbaceous Plants for Computer Imagery Purposes', *Computer Graphics*, Vol. 22, No. 4, pp. 141–150, 1988.

Woodcock, A., and M. Davis, *Catastrophe Theory*, Penguin Books, Harmondsworth, 1978.

Exercises

1. Notice that in each iteration shown in Fig. 7.4, the midpoint has been displaced randomly by a limited amount to produce a new corner that is either concave or convex. There is no problem with convex corners, but excessive displacements producing concave corners will eventually generate a self-intersecting shape.

   Write a procedure that initially stores the vertices of an equilateral triangle. At each iteration, the midpoint of each side is to be displaced by a random amount perpendicular to the ancestor line. The perpendicular displacement is not to exceed one eighth of the length of the ancestor line.

2. If necessary, recode the self-square program into a language for which you have a compiler available. Test out the program by guessing suitable values of lambda and z.

3. The nine lines superimposed on the map below can approximate the Isle of Wight. Try to devise a stochastic process that will give a reasonable approximation to the outline of the island within six iterations.

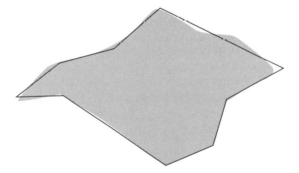

4. Find 'filled in' Julia sets that have a vertical and a horizontal axis of symmetry. Is there any pattern to the values of λ for such symmetrical sets?

5. Select a particularly attractive or unusual part of the Mandelbrot set. Modify the program shown in Fig. 7.15 so that only this region is displayed and it fills the whole of the viewport.

CHAPTER 8

Solid modelling

8.1 **Introduction**

One of the definitions of the word 'model' in the *Concise Oxford Dictionary* is:

**'A simplified (often mathematical) description of a system etc.,
to assist calculations and predictions.'**

Hence, when we set up a mathematical description of a solid object, we take these objectives into account.

These are some of calculations that we may wish to perform:

- the volume of the solid,
- its surface area,
- the position of its centroid,
- its moments of inertia about various axes,
- its mass.

We may wish to make the following predictions:

- how it would deform when subjected to specified loads.
- how it would move when subjected to specified forces.
- how heat would be conducted when subjected to specified thermal loads.
- how if would appear to a viewer at a specified position when illuminated by certain light sources.
- the visible effects that it has on other components in its environment, e.g. light reflection and refraction.

Clearly, the model must provide an accurate description of the geometry of the solid object, but will that be sufficient? To compute its mass, we would have to assume a value for its (uniform) density. For deformations, we need information on its modulus of elasticity. Visual effects are determined by the optical nature of the material and by the texture of the surfaces of the solid. Therefore, we can state that the fundamental purpose of a solid model is to provide an accurate description of the geometry. In addition, it must be possible to specify a wide range of secondary characteristics, in order to facilitate predictions for scientific and engineering applications, and for computer graphics.

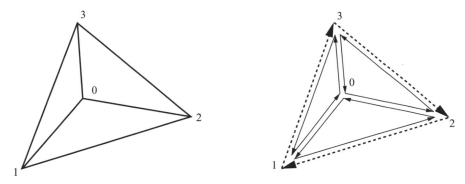

Figure 8.1 Surfaces of a tetrahedron.

8.2 **Boundary representation (B-rep)**

Essentially, this technique models the surface of a solid object by describing the geometry of its skin. One very useful type of solid object is the polyhedron. It may be considered to be a solid object bounded entirely by flat polygonal surfaces. We have already looked at a data structure for polygons: a geometry array and a connectivity array. We noted that disjoint circuits of edge vectors must represent a 3D cross section, and stated the convention that the inside is to the *left* of the vector direction. This convention needs to be redefined slightly for polygons that bound solid objects:

> *As seen from OUTSIDE the solid object,*
> *the surface is to the left of the vector direction.*

The simplest solid object is a tetrahedron. Its normal appearance is as above left, and it has four triangular bounding surfaces. The four triangles have been displaced slightly on the right of Fig. 8.1 for clarity.

You are looking at the *outside* of triangles **012**, **023**, and **031** and the edge vectors run around in an anti-clockwise direction with surface material to the *left* of the vectors. Imagine that the object is made of a transparent material and that you are looking through it at the *inside* of triangle **321** (shown with dotted lines). Hence the edge vectors run in a clockwise direction.

Of course, now that we are dealing with 3D objects each vertex has X, Y and Z coordinates. These can be stored in a 3-column array of real numbers such as this.

Vertex No.	X	Y	Z
0	3.25	5.20	2.75
1	0.00	0.00	5.50
2	6.50	0.00	5.50
3	3.25	0.00	0.75

The connectivity array (using the above convention) will be

Start	Finish
0	1
1	2
2	0
0	2
2	3
3	0
0	3
3	1
1	0
3	2
2	1
1	3

The above data structure can be classified as follows:

> **An edge is a function of a start vertex and a finish vertex,
> and a surface is a function of a set of *n* edges.**
>
> Symbolically, $\qquad E = f(V_0, V_1)$
>
> $\qquad\qquad\qquad\qquad S = f(E_1, E_2, \ldots, E_n)$

There are two other practicable data structures:

> **A surface is a function of a set of *n* vertices,
> and an edge is a function of two intersecting surfaces.**
>
> Symbolically, $\qquad S = f(V_1, V_2, \ldots, V_n)$
>
> $\qquad\qquad\qquad\qquad E = f(S_0, S_1)$

> **A surface is a function of a set of *n* vertices,
> and an edge is a function of a start vertex and a finish vertex.**
>
> Symbolically, $\qquad S = f(V_1, V_2, \ldots, V_n)$
>
> $\qquad\qquad\qquad\qquad E = f(V_0, V_1)$

The choice of a suitable data structure is a difficult one. The most important criterion is generally the nature of the application. The first data structure

$$E = f(V_0, V_1); \ S = f(E_1, E_2, \ldots, E_n)$$

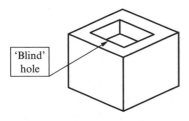

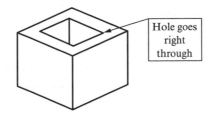

Figure 8.2a   Figure 8.2b

is suitable for a widely-used algorithm for rendering visible surfaces. There are other operations (e.g. geometric properties) that are more readily implemented using a different scheme.

The mathematician Euler showed that there is a fixed relationship between the number of vertices V, the number of edges E, and the number of surfaces S, of a polyhedron. Consider the following table of shapes:

Polyhedron	V	E	S	$V - E + S$
Tetrahedron	4	6	4	2
Pyramid	5	8	5	2
Cuboid	8	12	6	2
Five sided prism	10	15	7	2
Six sided prism	12	18	8	2
Fig. 8.2a	16	24	11	3
Fig. 8.2b	16	24	10	2

If you count and check the values in the above table, you will notice that, when the object has a blind hole, the relationship

$$V - E + S = 2$$

does *not* apply.

Euler's topological equation has to be modified to take account of the number of holes, H, and the number of holes that pass right through the object, I. Some solid models have separate parts, and the number of such parts, P, also has to be taken into account. The modified equation states that

$$V - E + S - H = 2(P - I)$$

Figure 8.2a has 16 vertices, 24 edges, 11 surfaces and 1 hole.
   Hence

$$V - E + S - H = 2$$

It has one part (hence, $P = 1$), and zero holes that go right through.

Therefore,

$$2(P - I) = 2$$

and the modified Euler equation is satisfied.

The modified Euler equation can be used as means of validating a data structure. In the above example for the tetrahedron, the number of vertices is simply the number of rows (4) in the geometry array. The number of edges is half the number of rows (6) in the connectivity array. Using Euler's equation, the number of surfaces can be computed as 4, and so there should be four distinct circuits of edges in the connectivity array. By inspection, it is clear that this is so.

The problem for the graphics programmer is to extract these circuits from the connectivity array. The problem is complicated by objects, such as those shown in Fig. 8.2, where one or more surfaces have two disjoint circuits. In other words, a circuit is not necessarily the same thing as a surface.

With the simple data structure we have examined thus far, it would only be possible to identify these multiple-circuit surfaces by showing that a set of vertices lies in the same plane, and that the circuits are disjoint. In other words, the connectivity array lacks useful information that can only be acquired at significant computational expense. Hence, a more sophisticated data structure is required and one very practicable choice is the linked list.

The topology of the object shown in Fig. 8.3 can be specified by the linked lists of vertices shown in the box.

Notice that it is now very simple to prove that the structure represents a solid object, once the edges have been counted correctly. An algorithm is needed which adds one to the tally of edges until the current circuit is completed. Hence, the first circuit of the top surface in Fig. 8.3 starts at Vertex No. 1, and so the increment is set equal to 1 until *after* the return to this start point.

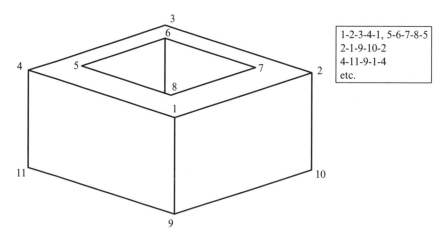

Figure 8.3 Object with surfaces specified by linked lists.

Link	Circuit Start Point	Increment	Edge Tally
1–2	1	1	1
2–3	1	1	2
3–4	1	1	3
4–1	1	1	4 (end of first circuit)
1–5	5	0	4
5–6	5	1	5
6–7	5	1	6
7–8	5	1	7
8–5	5	1	8

With such a data structure, it is possible to render (display) each surface accurately. However, most solid objects are opaque, and the surfaces nearest to the viewer hide (either partially or entirely) those that are further away. Therefore, the rendering of an opaque, concave polyhedron is no trivial task and calls for a so-called 'visible surface algorithm' of some complexity.

8.3 Constructive solid geometry (CSG)

There are two fundamental concepts that will be defined first.

1. A parametrised solid object is a simple (or 'primitive') object such as a cuboid, cylinder, or sphere. A primitive object can be positioned in 3D and have its dimensions specified using only a few real numbers. Position in 3D requires three real numbers. A cuboid has length, width, and height and hence three more real numbers are necessary, giving a total of six for this primitive. A cylinder has radius and length, giving a total of five parameters for this primitive. A sphere has only radius and hence requires just four parameters to define it completely. Because they are so useful in engineering design, other primitives such as the right cone, the wedge, and the fillet radius have been devised. The last two are not true primitives, as they have to be generated by differencing two more fundamental shapes. Hence, the term 'building block' is sometimes employed by vendors of CSG packages.

   Some CSG theorists regard the 'half space' as the true primitive. Figure 6.2 (page 65) shows how the normal vector to a plane is related to its homogeneous coordinates. Imagine that the plane is infinite in extent with solid matter on one side and empty space on the other – that is a half space.

   If two perpendicular half spaces are defined and an intersection operation is carried out, then the solid has one infinitely long edge with a right angle between the two surfaces. The intersection of three mutually perpendicular half spaces forms a solid right angle. If such a solid right angle

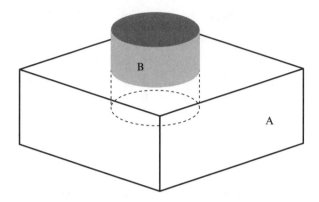

Figure 8.4 Primitives for difference operation.

is then intersected by another with the opposite orientation, then the result is a cuboid. The six leaves of the tree structure shown in Fig. 8.6 illustrate this concept.

2. Boolean operations in 3D are defined in the same manner as those that were specified for 2D on page 38. For example, the Difference **A** – **B** (where **A** and **B** are solid objects, not necessarily primitives) is the object, every atom of which lies inside **A** and *does not* lie within **B**. Hence, if **A** were a cuboid and **B** were a cylinder (see Fig. 8.4) the difference operation is analogous to a metal cutting process performed by a cylindrical cutter creating a hole in a block of metal. It is this convenient analogy that makes the CSG technique popular with 3D designers, because while they are specifying a shape they are also describing a technique by which it could be fabricated.

It is easy to comprehend that the algorithms that have to be designed for the 3D Boolean operations are far from simple. If a CSG modelling package makes available only the above three primitives, then it is still necessary to have twenty-one robust algorithms to carry out the following operations.

Cuboid A ∪ Cuboid B; Cuboid A ∩ Cuboid B; Cuboid A – Cuboid B

Cylinder A ∪ Cylinder B; Cylinder A ∩ Cylinder B; Cylinder A – Cylinder B

Sphere A ∪ Sphere B; Sphere A ∩ Sphere B; Sphere A – Sphere B

Cuboid A ∪ Cylinder B; Cuboid A ∩ Cylinder B;
Cuboid A – Cylinder B; Cylinder A – Cuboid B

Cuboid A ∪ Sphere B; Cuboid A ∩ Sphere B;
Cuboid A – Sphere B; Sphere A – Cuboid B

Cylinder A ∪ Sphere B; Cylinder A ∩ Sphere B;
Cylinder A – Sphere B; Sphere A – Cylinder B

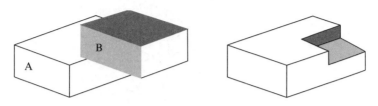

Figure 8.5 Difference operation carried out on boundary.

The above twenty-one operations are generally carried out by computing the boundary representations of the result. For example, each of the cuboids shown in Fig. 8.5 has a B-rep model that comprises six rectangular surfaces. The operation **Cuboid A – Cuboid B** will, because of the relative positions of the two primitives, produce a solid with nine flat surfaces, five of which are visible on the right of the figure.

A solid modelling package that could only carry out Boolean operations on primitive shapes would not be of much practical use. It is essential that the software can carry out Boolean operations on two solid objects which are themselves the result of previous such operations. For example, a 3D designer may wish to do further operations on the shape shown on the right of Fig. 8.5 so as to have a cylindrical hole which starts from one of the three new surfaces that were created from the earlier Boolean operation.

All of which tends to the conclusion that CSG is a very useful concept for the *ultimate user* of a software package. Moreover, the data structure is very efficient, as it is only necessary to store up to six real numbers for each primitive, an integer code for each type of primitive, and a binary tree structure for the operations. Each leaf in the tree is a 'primitive', which may be either a half space, a single geometric entity (cuboid, cylinder, sphere, cone), or a building block such as a wedge or fillet radius. Each node represents a Boolean operation. The root of the tree is the final CSG model. An example of such a tree is given in Fig. 8.6.

Because there is at least one natural analogy between CSG and manufacturing processes (difference ≡ metal cutting), it was inevitable that other operations would be devised. One such has been dubbed 'gluing', which is a simplified union operation that can only be carried out on objects that have a common interface surface: they touch, but do not intersect. The gluing operation is analogous to welding or bonding. Other 'operations' have been introduced for certain CAD packages. The so-called 'sectioning' operation is actually carried out by differencing a half space from the CSG model. Ever since the Industrial Revolution, sectional views have been draughted in order to make it easier to comprehend an engineering drawing. Naturally, the automatic generation of a sectional view is seen as a useful facility even if the manufacturing process is to be carried out using computer-controlled machine tools.

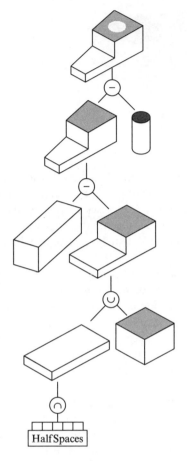

Figure 8.6 Binary tree for constructive solid geometry.

From the point of view of the software engineer, the implementation of Boolean operations is a formidable task. Historically, CSG took at least ten years to move from a doctoral thesis to commercial exploitation.

8.4 Modulated cross-sections

The data structure used so far has been classified symbolically as

$$E = f(V_0, V_1)$$
$$S = f(E_1, E_2, \ldots, E_n)$$

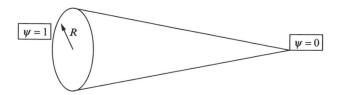

Figure 8.7 Linear modulation of a circle.

It has already been pointed out that CSG and B-rep are but two of several ways of representing a solid object. Another method is to modulate (mathematically) a cross section through a specified range of a defined parameter. Instead of describing the general case and then looking at particular examples, we will examine a particular example first, and then look at the general formulation.

Consider a circular cross-section with its centre at the origin of the x and y axes. The circle may be defined in terms of its radius r and an angle θ that varies from $-\pi$ to $+\pi$:

$$x = r \cos \theta, \quad y = r \sin \theta$$

subject to boundary conditions $-\pi \le \theta \le \pi$.

Suppose that there is some parameter ψ which varies between 0 and 1, and that r is a function of this parameter such that $r = R\psi$. The radius of the circular cross section varies linearly from 0 to R and the three equations together with their constraints describe a right cone of base radius R, as illustrated in Fig. 8.7.

A simple 2D shape may be defined parametrically by a 2-element column vector:

$$h(\omega) = \begin{bmatrix} h_1(\omega) \\ h_2(\omega) \end{bmatrix} \quad \text{with limits } \omega_0 \le \omega \le \omega_1$$

For example, an ellipse has the parametric equations

$$x = a \cos \theta \quad y = b \sin \theta$$

hence

$$h(\theta) = \begin{bmatrix} a \cos \theta \\ a \sin \theta \end{bmatrix} \quad \text{with limits } 0 \le \theta \le 2\pi$$

If another curve, oriented perpendicular to the first, is defined by

$$m(\eta) = \begin{bmatrix} m_1(\eta) \\ m_2(\eta) \end{bmatrix} \quad \text{with limits } \eta_0 \le \eta \le \eta_1$$

then the second curve can modulate the first, and the spherical product of the two curves defines the solid $x = m \otimes h$, which, by definition of the spherical product, is

$$x(\eta, \omega) = \begin{bmatrix} m_1(\eta)h_1(\omega) \\ m_1(\eta)h_2(\omega) \\ m_2(\eta) \end{bmatrix} \quad \text{with limits } \eta_0 \leq \eta \leq \eta_1; \ \omega_0 \leq \omega \leq \omega_1$$

This defines any point on the surface of the solid as having the coordinates

$$x = m_1(\eta)h_1(\omega) \quad y = m_1(\eta)h_2(\omega) \quad z = m_2(\eta)$$

8.4.1 *Superquadrics*

At first sight there would appear to be a serious disadvantage with the above technique for defining solids. Namely, the cross-section is defined by a single mathematical expression and may not allow sufficient flexibility to the creative 3D designer. However there are mathematical 2D forms which facilitate a wide range of shapes, and they should not unduly inhibit form design.

One very useful form is the *superellipse*. A normal ellipse has these equations and constraints:

$$x = a \cos \theta$$

$$y = b \sin \theta \quad \text{with limits } -\pi \leq \theta \leq \pi$$

Note that a circle (radius r) is a special case of an ellipse when $a = b = r$.

A superellipse gets its name from the fact that the trigonometrical functions are raised to a power (exponent) and hence there is a superscripted term in the equations. The equations are:

$$x = a \cos^e \theta$$

$$y = b \sin^e \theta$$

with boundary conditions $-\pi \leq \theta \leq \pi$

Of course, when $e = 1$ the superellipse is just a regular ellipse. When e is either less than or greater than one, we get the most interesting and usable cross-sections. The range of shapes is illustrated in Fig. 8.8.

A superquadric is generated by modulating a superellipse, or a superhyperbola. Figure 8.9 has been drawn using a modulating function:

$$m(\varphi) = \begin{bmatrix} \sin\varphi \\ 200\varphi \end{bmatrix}$$

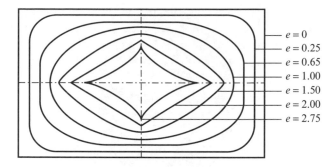

Figure 8.8 Qualitative effect on superellipse of various exponents.

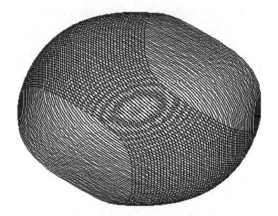

Figure 8.9 Modulated superellipse forming a superquadric.

The effect of this modulation will be that the x and y values are scaled by $\sin \varphi$ and the z value is equal to 200φ. The exponent of the superellipse is $e = 0.65$. Therefore the defining equations are:

$$x = a \sin \varphi \cos^{0.65} \theta \quad y = b \sin \varphi \sin^{0.65} \theta \quad z = 200\,\varphi$$

with limits $\pi/4 \leq \varphi \leq 3\pi/4$; $\qquad\qquad 0 \leq \theta \leq 2\pi$

Figure 8.9 was generated by incrementing φ in steps of $\pi/128$ through its range. The sections are sufficiently close together to give some idea of the solid shape, but it is only an impression that is spoiled by the Moiré fringe effect. We will address the question of how to obtain realistic images in Chapter 11.

8.5 Octrees

The octree encoding procedure for a 3D space is an extension of a scheme for 2D space called 'quadtree encoding'. A quadtree is a tree structure in which a

Figure 8.10 Frame for quadtree encoding.

parent node has four children. Figure 8.10 shows a square frame around a face-mask, the height of the square being exactly equal to the height of the face.

The convention that will be used for indicating the occupancy of a particular node is:

0 = empty

1 = full

2 = partially full

The root of the quadtree is the square that bounds the image, and it is clearly partially full. Hence the root node of the quadtree is marked with a 2. A quadtree is grown by dividing *only* partially full nodes into four quadrants, each of which may be empty, full, or partially full. For Fig. 8.10, the root node is partially full and so it is divided into the four quadrants shown in Fig. 8.11.

An empty node or a full node is a *leaf* node and is *not* subdivided. A partially full node is subdivided into quadrants. Of course, this process cannot continue indefinitely and so the process stops when the pixel level has been reached. For

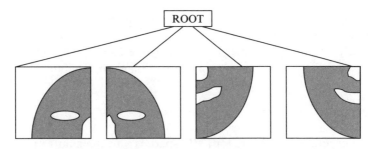

Figure 8.11 Partially full root node subdivided into four quadrants.

this reason, the enclosing square must have dimensions that are integer powers of two. If the pixel level is reached down any branch of the tree then, as a single pixel can only be visible or not visible, every such leaf will be either 0 or 1; it cannot contain a 2.

The quadtree is rendered by completely filling every quadrant whose node is recorded as full. Of course, this means that all the material contained within the boundary will appear exactly the same: there are no halftones. In other words, the quadtree technique is merely an alternative way of storing 2D shapes; it is *not* a method for storing a realistic image, such as the human face. Nevertheless, the technique can be adapted and extended so as to record square components that have the same greyscale.

For a solid object, an *octree* is required. The object is put into the cubic space that bounds its greatest dimension. In general, the object will only partially fill the cubic space. The space is then bisected in each direction, giving eight smaller cubes, each having one eighth of the volume of the parent. The eight new volumes are then examined and marked as empty, full or partial. Any partially full cubes are then divided into eight, and the tree may grow as far as a leaf that is a unit cube.

Hence, the process is very similar for both the 2D and the 3D case. As it is less complicated, we will consider how to render a basic quadtree. To do so, it is necessary to compute the position and size of each node containing 1. If the root of the tree is a (partially full) square of side 1024 (N) pixels then it is convenient to record its origin at the top left corner.

The coordinates of the top left are (0, 0), and the coordinates of the bottom right are ($N - 1$, $N - 1$). It is algebraically convenient to designate the root of the quadtree as level $L = 0$. Hence the only square at level 0 has a side of $N/2^0 = 1024$ pixels; the four squares at level 1 have sides of $N/2^1 = 512$ pixels. Any squares at level 2 will have sides of $N/2^2 = 256$ pixels, etc.

Similarly, the position of the top left corner of a quadrant depends upon the level and the parent node. It is convenient to order the positions of the four quadrants in a clockwise manner starting with that at the top left, as in Fig. 8.11. Hence, the only square at level 0 has its top left corner at (0, 0). The four squares at level 1 have their top left corners at ($0, 0$), ($N/2^1, 0$), ($N/2^1 1, N/2^1$), ($0, N/2^1$).

Generalising, if the top left corner of a parent node at level L is at (I, J) then the corners of child nodes at level $L + 1$ are at:

$$(I, J), (I + N/2^{L+1}, J), (I + N/2^{L+1}, J + N/2^{L+1}), (I, J + N/2^{L+1})$$

It is essential to record the top left corner of each node containing 1 (full) and each partially full node. The former can be rendered immediately, and the latter will be sub-divided into four child nodes. These child nodes are labelled 0... 3 for computing convenience. Thus, the upper left child is the zeroth child, and the lower left child is the third child.

Figure 8.12 is a letter **G**, formed by selecting pixels from an 8 × 8 grid. At each level, we count the number of set pixels. At level 0, 35/64 pixels are set, so

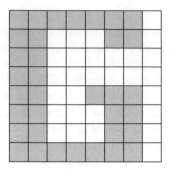

Figure 8.12 G shape in an 8 × 8 grid.

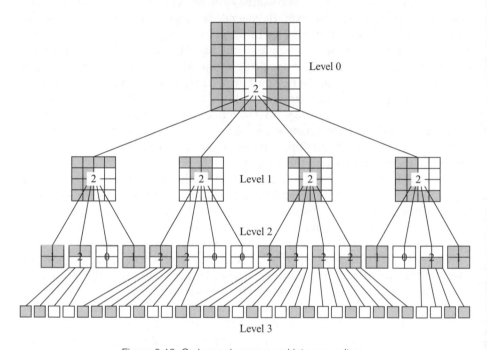

Figure 8.13 G shape decomposed into a quadtree.

the square is partially full and its node value is 2. At level 1, the zeroth child (at top left) has 10/16 pixels set: node value 2. The first child (top right) has 5/16 set: node value 2. The second child (bottom right) has 10/16 set: node value 2. The third child (bottom left) has 10/16 set: node value 2.

At level 2, the zeroth and the third child of the zeroth child of level 1 has 4/4 pixels set and so their node value is 1. Using quadtree encoding, the tree would be decomposed and encoded as shown in Fig. 8.13.

However, there is absolutely no point in storing the above tree in a computer file or memory. The main objection to doing so is the large amount of redundant information, i.e. every **2** merely indicates that a square is partially full and hence the children of the node must be examined. A secondary objection is the difficulty of computing the *position* of a full square. Hence, one storage technique is to record the *level* of a linked list of squares and then set up a list that contains an integer for the position followed by a Boolean variable that takes the value 1 when it is full.

Notice that there could be (and in fact are) sixteen values (0–15) in level 2. Listing only the non-2 values gives the linked list:

2,0 – 3,1 – 6,0 – 7,0 – 12,1 – 13,0

Similarly, there could be sixty-four values (0...63) in level 3. By analysing the children of squares that are partially full, we would get the linked list at this level. However, there is no point in recording empty squares. The shape can be correctly rendered by setting the entire level 0 square to empty, and then filling (or setting) those squares listed as full. As only full squares are listed, there is no need to record the fact that they are full. All that need be recorded for level 2 are the addresses:

0, 3, 12, 15

Level 3 becomes:

4, 5, 16, 17, 18, 20, 23, 32, 33, 34, 36, 39, 40, 43, 45, 46, 47, 58, 59

The only remaining problem is to associate a square number with the co-ordinates of its top-left corner. We can easily find the parent of a square by integer division by 4. Looking at the level 3 list above, we see that square no. 39 is to be filled. Its level 2 parent is the result of integer division 39/4 = 9. Notice that square no. 9 does not appear in the level 2 list, because, of course, as a parent it cannot be full. Looking at the quadtree, observe that the children of each **2** node are designated 0–3 and square 39 is the 3rd child of its parent. We can find the child number using modulo (or remainder) arithmetic. 39/4 = 9, *remainder 3*.

The top left corner of the level 0 square is (0, 0) and its four children have their corners at:

(0, 0), (1 + *N*/2, 0), (1 + *N*/2, 1 + *N*/2), (0, 1 + *N*/2)

One technique is to work back to a level 1 grandparent and compute the top left corner of the grandchild. A better technique is to pre-compute the coordinates for each level, then simply look up the coordinates of the squares that are filled. For the present example, a list of 1 + 4 + 16 + 64 = 85 pairs would be generated.

By slightly enhancing the method of data storage, it can be used for recording images other than the 'line art' type that we have just examined. A somewhat more realistic image can be built using a grey scale with the range 0...3:

0 = white

1 = light grey

2 = dark grey

3 = black

It will generally be the case that there are some such uniformly coloured square clusters. Hence, the quadtree technique will be a significantly more efficient way to record the total image than the obvious solution of recording the greyscale of each of the 1024 pixels. A similar enhancement can be applied to octree encoding in order to distinguish between component parts of a solid object.

8.6 **Summary**

- A solid model is, fundamentally, a mathematical description of the *geometry* of a solid object. If the modelling technique allows other characteristics of the object to be recorded, then the model can be used for a wide range of applications, in addition to computer graphics.
- Boundary representation is a technique whereby the solid is defined in terms of its bounding surfaces. The component surfaces may be of any mathematical form and each such component will share common edges with adjacent surfaces. The fact of edge sharing enables a newly created data structure to be validated. The structure must also obey the modified Euler topological equation, which takes account of holes in the object.
- Constructive solid geometry is a technique whereby primitive solid objects (such as cuboids, cylinders, and spheres) are combined using the modified Boolean operations of Union, Intersection, and Difference. The primitive objects are the leaves of a binary tree, the Boolean operators are the nodes, and the root of the tree is the complete solid model. It follows that many of the Boolean operations will be carried out on a pair of objects, one or both of which are not a primitive. Hence, the necessary algorithms are very sophisticated, and they work by converting the CSG model into the corresponding B-rep model.
- A modulated cross section model has each cross section defined as a function of a single parameter ω. The modulation is a function of another parameter η and the solid object is the spherical product of the modulating function and the cross section function:

$$x(\eta, \omega) = \begin{bmatrix} m_1(\eta)h_1(\omega) \\ m_1(\eta)h_2(\omega) \\ m_2(\eta) \end{bmatrix}$$

Although the cross section is a function of only one parameter, some interesting and attractive solids can be generated by using certain mathematical forms, such as the superellipse and the superhyperbola.

- At the root of an octree is the complete solid object. Unless the object is itself a cube, then the cubic space bounding it will only be partially full of material. Any such partially full cubic space has eight children, each of which may either be full, empty, or partially full. Only partially full cubic spaces have children, and the leaves of the octree are cubes of a size equal to the minimum specified for the application. In practice, the availability of high-quality B-rep modelling systems has limited the use of quadtree encoding to a small number of specialised applications.

8.7 **Further reading**

For greater detail of the application of some of the mathematics presented in this chapter, the following are recommended.

Anand, V. B., *Computer Graphics and Geometric Modeling for Engineers*, John Wiley and Sons, 1993.

Barr, A. H., 'Superquadrics and Angle-Preserving Transformations', *IEEE Computer Graphics and Applications*, Vol. 1, No. 1, pp. 11–23, 1981.

Barsky, B. A., 'A Description and Evaluation of Various 3D Models', *IEEE Computer Graphics and Applications*, Vol. 4, No. 1, pp. 38–52, 1984.

Braid, I. C., Hillyard, R. C. and I. A. Stroud, *Stepwise Construction of Polyhedra in Geometric Modelling*, Mathematical Methods in Computer Graphics and Design (Ed. Brodlie, K. W.), Academic Press, 1980.

Braid, I. C., *Designing with Volumes (Second Edition)*, Cantab Press, 1974. Based upon Braid's Cambridge University thesis, this work demonstrated conclusively that Constructive Solid Geometry was practicable for 3D design.

Mortenson, M. E., *Geometric Modelling*, John Wiley and Sons, 1997. The second edition, which reflects advances since the mid-1980s. It focuses on the practice of geometric modelling.

Piegl, L., *Fundamental Developments in Computer-Aided Geometric Modelling*, Academic Press London, 1993. Covers all important aspects of geometric modelling. The historical overview is combined with an analysis of recent developments.

Exercises

1. Is the following B-rep data a valid solid model?

Vertex	x	y	z
1	10.0	10.0	19.0
2	10.0	10.0	10.0
3	10.0	23.0	10.0
4	10.0	23.0	19.0
5	32.0	10.0	19.0
6	32.0	10.0	15.0
7	14.0	10.0	19.0
8	14.0	13.0	19.0
9	20.0	23.0	19.0
10	20.0	10.0	19.0
11	14.0	10.0	17.0
12	14.0	13.0	17.0
13	20.0	13.0	17.0
14	20.0	10.0	17.0

Edge	Start	Finish
1	1	2
2	2	3
3	3	4
4	4	1
5	5	6
6	6	3
7	2	6
8	4	5
9	1	7
10	7	8
11	8	9
12	9	10
13	10	5
14	8	12
15	7	11
16	9	13
17	10	14
18	11	14
19	14	13
20	13	12
21	12	11

Surface	Edge vectors
1	−1, −4, −3, −2
2	3, 8, 5, 6
3	−6, −7, 2
4	9, 10, 11, 12, 13, −8, 4
5	−13, 17, −18, −15, −9, 17, −5
6	15, −21, −14, −10
7	−17, −12, 16, −19
8	19, 20, 21, 18
9	−11, 14, −20, −16

Sketch the object that is represented. Use the modified Euler equation to check if the relationship between vertices, edges, and surfaces is correct. Check manually if every edge appears twice, in opposite directions, in the list of edge vectors.

Write a simple program that will carry out the same check and find out if the results agree with the manual method. If the data is not a valid model, your program should reformat the list of surfaces to make it so.

2. Figure 8.5 shows one cuboid differenced from another. A procedure to carry out this operation has first to convert each parametrised shape into a set of six rectangular surfaces. Write a program that accepts two sets of six real numbers representing the size and position of each cuboid. The program is then to decompose each cuboid into a B-rep structure, and print out a table of vertices, edges, and surfaces.

3. Having completed question 2, design a procedure that will compute all the valid intersections of the surfaces of the two cuboids and then determine the difference between the two cuboids. Bear in mind that there are fifteen possible intersections and a valid intersection will create a new edge, which needs to be stored as part of a new object. Finally, the new object should be validated using Euler's equation.

4. Write a program that will accept values of a, b, and e and then draw a superellipse using the equations:

$$x = a \cos^e\theta$$

$$y = b \sin^e\theta$$

5. Having completed question 4, experiment with various modulations of the superellipse, and display an isometric view of the resulting solid.

6. A cube of side 32 mm is differenced from a cube of side 64 mm. The relative positions of the two cubes in the xy plane are shown below and the z position is such that the depth of the hole formed in the larger cube is 16 mm.

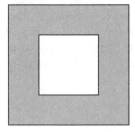

Draw the complete octree for this object. At what level in the tree is every node either full or empty? Outline an algorithm that could carry out the octree encoding automatically.

CHAPTER 9

The visible surface problem

9.1 **Introduction**

The 'visible surface problem' arises when a solid object is to be displayed in a realistic manner. Throughout this chapter, the same concave polyhedron will illustrate the various techniques. The object has been designed so that most aspects of the visible surface problem can be examined, and it is illustrated in Fig. 9.1. It has been dubbed 'the stepped wedge' for ease of reference. The reader is recommended to make a model of the stepped wedge from card, by carefully tracing the flat shape shown in Fig. 9.2, then cutting, folding and gluing the card together, as indicated. The topic treated in this chapter is a particularly difficult one, and a simple 3D model should significantly assist the learning process.

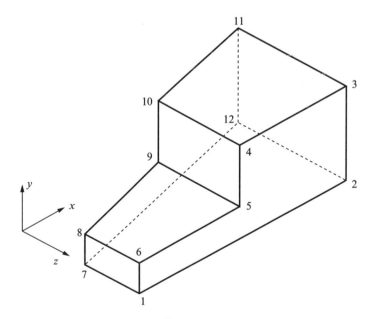

Figure 9.1 The stepped wedge.

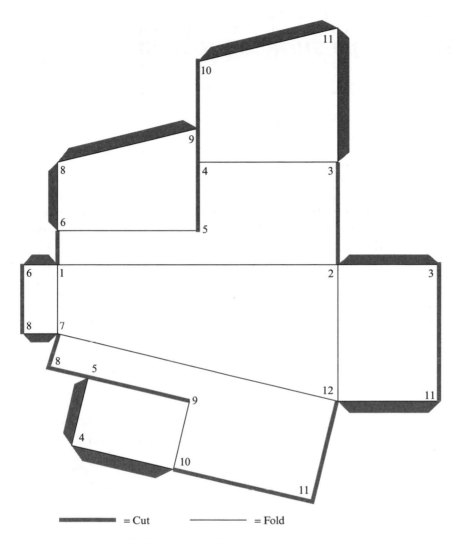

Figure 9.2 Outline of the card for a model of the stepped wedge.

The B-rep data structure for the stepped wedge is shown in Fig. 9.3.

Notice how the object is been defined by the above arrays. The representation used (see page 96) is that an edge is a function of a start vertex and a finish vertex

$$E = f(V_0, V_1)$$

and a surface is a function of a set of edges

$$S = f(E_1, E_2, \ldots, E_n)$$

Vertex	X	Y	Z	Edge	Start	Finish
1	0.00	0.00	80.00	1	1	2
2	160.00	0.00	80.00	2	2	3
3	160.00	60.00	80.00	3	3	4
4	80.00	60.00	80.00	4	4	5
5	80.00	20.00	80.00	5	5	6
6	0.00	20.00	80.00	6	6	1
7	0.00	0.00	40.00	7	7	8
8	0.00	20.00	40.00	8	8	9
9	80.00	20.00	20.00	9	9	10
10	80.00	60.00	20.00	10	10	11
11	160.00	60.00	0.00	11	11	12
12	160.00	0.00	0.00	12	12	7
				13	1	7
				14	6	8
				15	5	9
				16	4	10
				17	3	11
				18	2	12

Surface	Edge vectors
1	1, 2, 3, 4, 5, 6
2	7, 8, 9, 10, 11, 12
3	13, −12, −18, −1
4	14, −7, −13, −6
5	15, −8, −14, −5
6	16, −9, −15, −4
7	17, −10, −16, −3
8	18, −11, −17, −2

Figure 9.3 B-rep data structure for the stepped wedge.

Referring to page 97, this object has $V = 12$, $E = 18$ and $S = 8$. There is only one part to the object and so $P = 1$. There are no holes and so $H = 0$ and $I = 0$. The modified Euler topological equation

$$V - E + S - H = 2(P - I)$$

therefore becomes

$$12 - 18 + 8 - 0 = 2 = 2(1 - 0)$$

and so the solid model passes the first test of validity. The second test of validity is that each edge appears twice in the list of surfaces, and in opposite directions. If you check down the list in Fig. 9.3, you will find that each of the eighteen edges appears twice, once positively and once negatively. Hence we have a valid boundary representation of a solid object and it is a 'model' in the technical sense. In other words, the model has all the geometric properties of the solid that it represents, and from the model it will be possible to compute such things as the volume of the object, its centre of gravity, its surface area, etc. In addition, if we assume that the material from which the object is made is opaque,

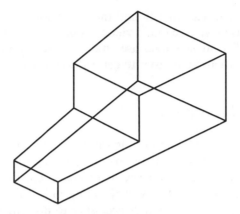

Figure 9.4 Wire frame representation of the stepped wedge.

then it will be possible to generate a correct rendering of the object as seen from any specified direction.

It is simple enough to generate a 'wire frame' representation of the object as seen from any angle. All that is required is a procedure to rotate the vertices around the three axes, plus a line drawing procedure to show the edges. The above table showing the relationship $S = f(E_1, E_2, \ldots, E_n)$ is *not* required in order to generate the wire frame. The result looks like that shown in Fig. 9.4.

Not only is the wire frame confusing, but it also has no 'depth cues' and so the viewer cannot determine whether it represents the object shown in Fig. 9.5a or 9.5b.

The only real advantage of 'wire frame' is that it is a quick, cheap way to indicate something about the appearance of a solid object. As the information

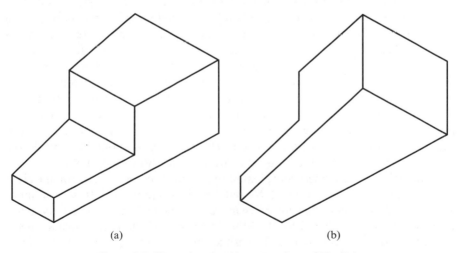

(a)   (b)

Figure 9.5 Alternative visual interpretations of Fig. 9.4.

provided about the surfaces that bound the object was *not* used in the generation of Fig. 9.2, it is inevitable that a viewer cannot comprehend the wire frame as a solid object. The surface data are vital, and we will now look at various ways in which they are used in order to get realistic images of a solid object.

9.2 **Painter's algorithm**

This technique is called the painter's algorithm because it resembles the way in which (some) artists build up a picture by first painting the background colours, then the most distant objects, then nearer ones, and so on. The last step is to paint the foreground objects, and they will therefore hide anything that is further away. In computer graphics, it is first necessary to do a depth sort of the surfaces, and store the furthest surface in some available frame buffer. The surface with the next furthest vertex is then processed, and the frame buffer is suitably modified. The process continues until all the surfaces have been processed.

There are, of course, many complicating factors to what looks like a simple emulation of the painter's technique. Some surfaces will overlap, and further processing is required in order to determine which parts of the overlapping surfaces are closer to the viewer. This complication arises frequently with complex scenes, but also with a single object that has even one concave (reentrant) corner. If this technique is applied to a single *convex* polyhedron, then the situation is simplified by the fact that there can be no ambiguity as to which surface to paint.

As a frame buffer is not always available to the application programmer, it has been necessary to develop other techniques, still using something of the artist's method. Suppose the painter has a building of some kind within his picture. The building is a solid object to be represented in two dimensions and the artist will paint those parts of the building that *face* the viewer and are *not hidden* by other features of the same building. Therefore, when rendering a solid model, if it can be shown that a surface is facing away from the viewer then it is of no further interest. Certainly, it need not be painted, because it is certain to be over-painted when the nearer surfaces are processed. Moreover, some surfaces can be very close to the viewer, and yet face in the wrong direction. It is a complete waste of effort to paint such surfaces, only to have them covered later.

To illustrate this point, it is first necessary to rotate the stepped wedge. To produce an 'isometric' view of an object, it is first rotated through +45° around the y axis, followed by a rotation of $\tan^{-1}(1/\sqrt{2})$, which is about 35°, around the x axis. This will transform the object coordinates as shown in Fig. 9.6.

Using these transformed coordinates, the normal vectors to each of the eight surfaces can be computed, using Newell's equations (page 70). It is essential to work around the edges of each surface *in the order prescribed by the data structure*. If the order is not adhered to, then the direction cosines of the normal vector could be wrongly computed, and a visible surface would be classed as hidden, or vice versa. Knowing the normal vector, the direction cosines can be computed.

X	Y	Z
56.57	−32.66	46.19
169.71	32.66	−46.19
169.71	81.65	−11.55
113.14	48.99	34.64
113.14	16.33	11.55
56.57	−16.33	57.74
28.28	−16.33	23.09
28.28	0.00	34.64
70.71	40.82	−23.09
70.71	73.48	−0.00
113.14	114.31	−57.74
113.14	65.32	−92.38

Figure 9.6 Object coordinates rotated for isometric view.

Surface No.	$\cos \alpha$	$\cos \beta$	$\cos \gamma$
1	0.71	−0.41	0.58
2	−0.86	0.30	−0.42
3	−0.00	−0.82	−0.58
4	−0.71	−0.41	0.58
5	0.00	0.82	0.58
6	−0.71	−0.41	0.58
7	0.00	0.82	0.58
8	0.71	0.41	−0.58

Figure 9.7 Direction cosines for the surfaces of the stepped wedge.

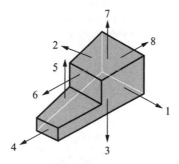

Figure 9.8 Normal vectors for the surfaces of the stepped wedge.

The only relevant direction cosine is $\cos \gamma$ (for the z axis) as this axis is the viewing direction. Therefore, a surface can be eliminated if the angle γ between its normal and the z axis is greater than 90°. Figure 9.7 shows the values obtained for each surface by using the transformed coordinates given in Fig. 9.7.

The normal vectors of the eight surfaces have been indicated in Fig. 9.8. As the angle between the normal vector and the z axis is greater than 90° (cosine is negative), then surfaces 2, 3 and 8 are *not* oriented in a direction that could be seen by a viewer looking into the z axis. Hence, they are not visible and their hidden edges are indicated with white lines in Fig. 9.8.

9.3 **Warnock's algorithm**

This was a method developed at Utah State University. It employs the classical 'divide and conquer' paradigm. It is convenient to think of the algorithm as having two slave procedures:

1. the object analyser,
2. the renderer.

Initially, the object analyser places a 2D projection of the solid model in a square frame whose dimensions are an integer power of two, as shown in Fig. 9.9.

This is akin to creating the root of a quadtree structure, as was explained on page 106. The object analyser 'asks' the renderer if it is able to process the contents of the current square. If the answer is 'yes', then the current square is rendered. If the answer is 'no' then the current square is divided into four and the four child squares are pushed onto a stack to await processing. For the current example, suppose that the top of the stack (Child 0 at Level 1) has come from the top left square of Fig. 9.9, as shown in Fig. 9.10. The top square is popped off the stack and the renderer is again asked if it can process the current square. If it again answers 'no', then the current square is further divided to give four smaller squares.

Once again, the top of the stack is popped, and the object analyser asks the renderer if it can deal with this smaller square. In this example, as shown in Fig. 9.11, the square is empty; so the reply would be 'yes' (there is nothing to be done).

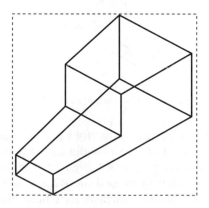

Figure 9.9 Square frame defines root of quadtree.

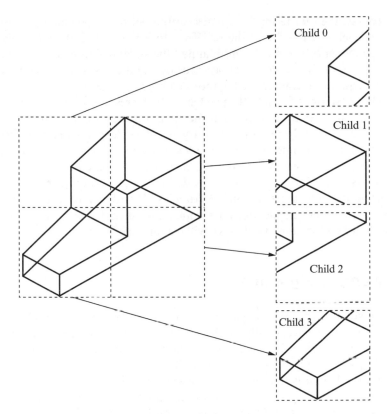

Figure 9.10 Level 1 children of the complete stepped wedge.

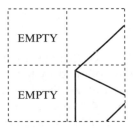

Figure 9.11 Two level 2 children that do not require subdivision.

This child has therefore been processed and is not further divided. The renderer may also be able to cope with Child 1, so that would not be divided either. Child 2 is more problematic, so it may well be further divided and its children pushed onto the stack. The 0th child of Child 2 is now at the top of the stack, and it would be the next to be popped and processed. Notice that these (grand)children will take precedence over Child 3, which could have been easily processed had it been at the top of the stack.

Of course, the quartering of squares cannot continue indefinitely. Eventually the pixel level is reached and the renderer does not have to be interrogated: a pixel is either set or not set. In this manner, the stack will ultimately be emptied. The rendering of the whole object proceeds by dealing first with the larger empty or simple squares, but many of the more complex first generation children may have to be taken right down to the pixel level. If the result is displayed in real time (not stored and displayed later) then the effect on the viewer is quite irritating. Furthermore, virtually all contemporary graphics displays are refreshed one horizontal line at a time, and not by selecting square areas in seemingly random positions. In other words, there is a serious mismatch between the shape of the units into which the scene is divided (in order to conquer) and the display technology. For these reasons, Warnock's algorithm was never adopted for commercial graphics applications. Its importance is that it pointed the way to a truly practical solution – one that we will examine next.

9.4 Scan line algorithm

Warnock showed that the 'divide-and-conquer' approach to the visible surface problem could be successfully implemented. A truly practicable solution was developed by dividing the scene not into smaller and smaller squares, but into rectangles, all of equal height and width. The width is the width of the display area, and the height is that of a pixel – a scan line. The fundamental method is to compute a cross-section of the solid model where it is intersected by a scan plane. We will treat a scan plane as a horizontal surface, and every point on the surface satisfies the equation:

$$y = Y \text{ (a constant).}$$

First, the stepped wedge is rotated to a position that is easy to process: a rotation of $+45°$ around the y axis, followed by $\tan^{-1}(1/\sqrt{2})$ around the x axis (see code on page 68). When viewed along the z axis, the solid shape appears as shown in Fig. 9.1. Surfaces No. 1, 4, 5, 6 and 7 are visible.

For the B-rep data structure shown on page 116, it is relatively easy to compute the cross-sectional shape at $y = Y$. The object has eighteen edges (all straight lines) and each is defined by its start point and its finish point. Let the start point of a selected edge be at (x_0, y_0, z_0), its finish point be at (x_1, y_1, z_1) and define a parameter t which varies from 0 at the start to 1 at the finish.

At any point (x, y, z) on the edge gives, by definition:

$$t = (y - y_0)/(y_1 - y_0) \quad \text{or} \quad y = y_0(1 - t) + y_1 t$$

The scan line will intersect this edge where $y = Y$.

At that point $t = (Y - y_0)/(y_1 - y_0)$.

Hence, in order to define a cross section of the object, it is first necessary to compute the value of t for each of the eighteen edges. If $0 \le t \le 1$ then the intersection is valid and the intersection point is one of the vertices of the cross-sectional polygon.

The next step is to join pairs of intersection points together, provided the intersected edges lie in the same surface. For example, suppose it was found that the scan plane has valid intersections with edges:

1   4   8   12   15

These five points could be connected in ten ways, only some of which are valid:

1	–	4	(In surface No. 1)
1	–	8	(Invalid)
1	–	12	(In surface No. 3)
1	–	15	(Invalid)
4	–	8	(Invalid)
4	–	12	(Invalid)
4	–	15	(In surface No. 6)
8	–	12	(In surface No. 2)
8	–	15	(In surface No. 5)
12	–	15	(Invalid)

Notice that a valid surface can appear only once in a list like the above. It is commonsense that a surface is either cut or not cut by the scan plane; it cannot be cut more than once. We now have the bounding lines of the cross-section. In order for it to be a valid cross-section of a solid object, the above set of valid line combinations must form one or more (disjoint) circuits. Inspecting the above list reveals that there is such a circuit when the intersections are joined in the following order.

1	–	4	(In surface No. 1)
4	–	15	(In surface No. 6)
15	–	8	(In surface No. 5)
8	–	12	(In surface No. 2)
12	–	1	(In surface No. 3)

Figure 9.12 shows three views, looking down the y axis, of the stepped wedge rotated to the isometric position. The left-hand view shows the complete object. The centre view shows the object sectioned through by a horizontal plane whose equation is $y = 100$. The resulting section is triangular. The right-hand view is a section for $y = 25$, and the resulting section is hexagonal. The minimum and

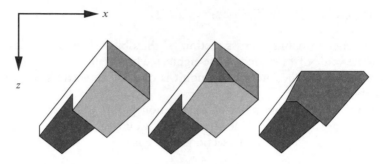

Figure 9.12 Looking down the *y* axis at sections of the stepped wedge.

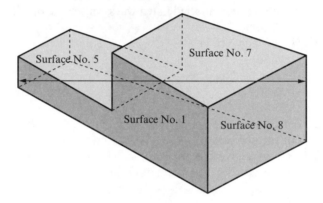

Figure 9.13 Stepped wedge with Surface No. 5 partially visible.

maximum values of y are on the boundary of the object, where the cross section has zero area, and would be rendered as a single pixel. As the z arrow points at the eyes of a person viewing this solid object, it is possible to select the surfaces to be rendered, and hence made visible to the viewer. In Fig. 9.13, it is the full lines that should be displayed and the dashed lines that must not be rendered.

In this case, the decisions that have to be made are simple, as a line across a surface either does or does not appear in its entirety. We will now rotate the stepped wedge to a position that is a severe test for any visible surface algorithm. As the object has been designed with one concave corner, there will be views when one of the surfaces forming the corner is partially hidden. Concave polyhedra defeat many simple visible surface algorithms because they generally rely on a surface being either wholly visible or invisible. If the stepped wedge is rotated $-45°$ around the y axis, followed by $\tan^{-1}(1/\sqrt{2})$ around the x axis, the solid shape looks like Fig. 9.13 when viewed along the z axis. Surface No. 5 is partially visible.

The problem presented to the scan line algorithm is to compute how much of certain scan lines should be rendered with the colour or texture of surface

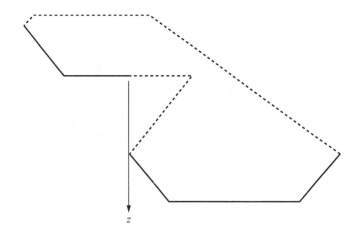

Figure 9.14 Section with Surface No. 5 partially visible.

no. 5, and how much with the characteristics of surface no. 1. If we examine one of the cross-sections that lies between vertex no. 6 and vertex no. 9, we get the circuit shown in Fig. 9.14.

The viewer should be presented only with those lines shown in bold in Fig. 9.13, as they are part of the surfaces that are nearest to the viewer and not hidden by nearer surfaces. The section is for the scan plane indicated by the double-headed arrow in Fig. 9.13. Comparing the two figures, it is possible to see how information taken from the cross-section enables the rendering to be done correctly.

Hence, the scan line algorithm provides the correct solution to the problem, but that does not necessarily make it practicable. If it were necessary to compute up to (say) 1024 cross-sections for a more complex object than we are looking at, then the computational cost would be very significant. Exploiting the phenomenon called 'scan line coherence' can reduce this cost.

Look again at the triangular section shown in Fig. 9.12. There will be many adjacent triangles for scan lines with the larger values of y. For a polyhedron, it is fairly obvious that there will always be a series of circuits with the same number of sides and these sides will be parallel. There is a significant change in the shape of the cross section only when the height of the scan plane passes from one side of a vertex to the other.

Therefore, there will generally be a series of polygons with the same number of sides and the variation in the length of the sides will be *linear*. As the height of an object vertex is known as soon as the object has been through a rotational transformation, it is only necessary to compute one cross-section that lies between two vertices, and then all other similar cross-sections can be derived by extrapolation.

Figure 9.15 shows two adjacent quadrilateral cross-sections. The corners of the quadrilateral lie on object edges (the arrowhead lines), and knowing the value of y for this section enables the computation

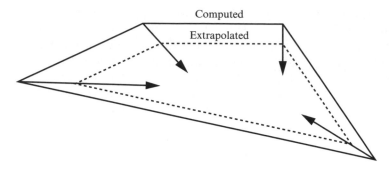

Figure 9.15 Adjacent sections by extrapolation.

$$t = (y - y_0)/(y_1 - y_0)$$

to be done for each of the four edges.

The (x, z) coordinates are readily computed from $x = x_0(1 - t) + x_1t$, etc. When y is incremented, a new value of t is computed, from which the new values of (x, z) are easily determined.

9.5 **Summary**

- A wire-frame rendering of the edges specified by a solid model can be done very quickly. Because edges that should be hidden from the viewer are actually visible the wire-frame rendering is at best confusing, and at worst ambiguous.
- The painter's algorithm is based upon the principle that, along any given line of sight, it is the part of the object, or scene nearest to the viewer, that can actually be seen. The most distant feature is rendered first and it may be then successively over-painted until the nearest, visible details have been rendered. Clearly, this is computationally expensive and the process may be speeded up by first computing the normal vectors of the surfaces that comprise the scene. Any normal vector that subtends an angle of more than 90° with the line of sight is that of a surface orientated away from the viewer and need not be painted. In general, concave polyhedra cannot be rendered correctly by this algorithm, as it is always possible for part of a surface to be hidden, whilst the remainder is visible.
- Warnock's algorithm employed the 'divide and conquer' paradigm. Rather like quadtree encoding, any square area of the scene that could not be rendered was divided into four squares that were pushed onto a last-in-first-out stack. The contents of the square at the top of the stack was examined and either rendered, if possible, or further subdivided if not. Subdivision ceases at the pixel level. The algorithm is important for its pioneering qualities, and also for pointing the way to more practicable methods.

- The scan line algorithm also employs a 'divide and conquer' paradigm. However, in this case the subdivision of the total scene is into rectangles that are one pixel high, and of the width of the display area. All objects within the scene are mathematically sectioned at a specific y value. The sectional view thus generated is inspected in order to discover the parts of the component surfaces that are closest to the viewer and not hidden by other surfaces. Pixels are set on the scan line accordingly. As the computational cost of extracting a sectional view is high, exploiting the concept of scan-line coherence can save time. Except at certain discontinuities, the pattern of pixels on one scan line is very much like the neighbouring lines, and it may often be advantageous to carry out an appropriate extrapolation process, instead of re-computing the cross-section.

9.6 **Further reading**

Details of the vast amount of research that has been devoted towards finding a practicable solution to the visible surface problem are to be found in the following books and papers.

Appel, A., 'The Notion of Quantitative Invisibility and the Machine Rendering of Solids', *Proc. ACM 1967 National Conference*, pp. 387–393, 1967.

Atherton, P. R , 'A Scan-Line Hidden Surface Removal Procedure for Constructive Solid Geometry', *Computer Graphics*, Vol. 17, No. 3, pp. 73–82, 1983.

Loutrel, P. P., 'A Solution to the Hidden Line Problem for Computer-drawn Polyhedra', *IEEE Trans. On Computers*, Vol. 18, No. 3, pp. 205–213, 1970.

Mahl, R., 'Visible Surface Algorithm for Quadric Patches', *IEEE Trans. On Computers*, C-21, pp. 1–4, Jan. 1972.

Newman, W. M. and R. F. Sproull, *Principles of Interactive Computer Graphics*, McGraw-Hill, New York, 1979.

Sutherland, I. E., R. F. Sproull, and R. A. Shumaker, *A Characterization of Ten Hidden Surface Algorithms*, Comput. Surveys, Vol. 6, No. 1, pp. 1–55, 1974.

Warnock, J., *A Hidden-Surface Algorithm for Computer-Generated Half-Tone Pictures*, Technical Report TR 4–15, NTIS AD-753 671, Computer Science Department, University of Utah, Salt Lake City, Utah, June 1969.

Wood, P. Y., and H. Freeman, 'A Procedure for Generating Visible Line Projections of Quadric Surfaces', *Proc. 1971 IFIP Congress*, North-Holland, 1971.

Exercises

1. Use a spreadsheet or write a simple program to validate the data given in Fig. 9.3. The modified topological equation must be satisfied and it must be shown that each edge appears twice in the list of surfaces, once positively and once negatively.

2. If you have the facilities available, make a cube of side 100 mm from wood or high-density foam. Saw or slice off one corner of the cube, as indicated below.

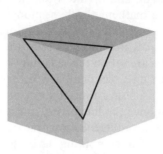

Remove the corner, and examine the cut section. Set up a B-rep model of the cube and rotate this model so that the cut surface is horizontal, i.e. it corresponds to a scan line. Write a program to compute the (x, z) coordinates of the triangular section. Check these coordinates against the physical model. Finally, enhance your program so that you can compute any section through the cube.

3. If you have not already done so, make up the model of the stepped wedge, using Fig. 9.2 as a template.

4. Physically rotate the model of the stepped wedge through $-45°$ around the y axis, followed by a rotation of about $-37°$ around the x axis. Mark the edges that are wholly or partially visible. Try to get the same result from a computer program. In other words, is it a simple matter to select (and clip) visible edges?

5. Use Fig. 9.14 as the current section, and write a program that will use scan-line coherence to determine the section that is one scan line above this one.

CHAPTER 10

Pixel mapping

10.1 Introduction

Practically all contemporary graphics are raster scan refreshed, and therefore pixel mapped. Hence, the most basic instruction that the programmer can give to a monochrome graphics display is to set a specified pixel. For some of the early raster scan displays, that was the only instruction available. The generation of more complex elements, such as lines, circles and text, all required software procedures. When desktop machines such as the Apple Macintosh and the IBM PC were introduced, such procedures were hardware generated. In other words, the programmer could now issue a command such as `Lineto` `(x, y)` and the line was drawn using a procedure from the machine's instruction set, which resides in the microprocessor.

Another very valuable type of procedure 'fills' a well-defined area of the display with pixels of the same colour or greyscale value. Again, the procedure is implemented in hardware in order to attain the necessary speed. One such algorithm is examined in detail below.

10.2 Bresenham's line algorithm

This line-generating algorithm uses only incremental integer calculations. The first step is to find the pixel position that is nearest to the start point of the line. Having established this starting position, there are eight different modes of selecting the next pixel, depending upon the gradient of the line. These octants are illustrated in Fig. 10.1.

Bresenham's algorithm does not have to cope with eight different cases, as the fundamental problem is always the same. The algorithm first decides the direction in which to draw the line. For a gradient $m \leq 1$, if the x coordinate of the specified start point is greater than the x coordinate of the finish point, then the 'start' point becomes the 'finish' point, and vice versa. The value of x will increase by one unit at each step. Such a procedure is suitable for octants 1, 4, 5 and 8 shown in Fig. 10.1. A different, but essentially similar, procedure is required to process lines in octants 2, 3, 6 and 7, where $m > 1$. In that case, the value of y will increase by one unit at each step.

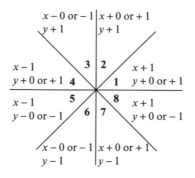

Figure 10.1 Octants for Bresenham's line algorithm.

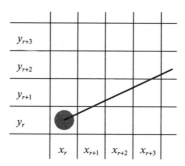

Figure 10.2 Choosing the pixel nearest to the line segment.

Figure 10.2 illustrates part of a pixel-mapped display screen where a straight line segment ($y = mx + k$) is to be drawn. The vertical axes show scan-line positions and the horizontal axes identify pixel columns. At unit x intervals, we need to decide which of two possible pixel positions is closer to the line path at each sample step.

Starting from the point shown in Fig. 10.2, we need to determine at the next position whether to plot the pixel at position (x_{r+1}, y_r) or at (x_{r+1}, y_{r+1}). In the first octant, there is always an increment of 1 in the x direction. In the y direction the increment is either 0 or 1. Starting at the left end (x_0, y_0), we step to each successive column and plot the pixel whose y value is closest to the line path.

If it has earlier been decided that the pixel at (x_r, y_r) is to be displayed, the next step is to determine which pixel to plot in column x_{r+1}. The choices are the pixels at positions $(x_r + 1, y_r)$ and $(x_r + 1, y_r + 1)$. In order to choose between the two candidate pixels, we compare the two vertical distances from the mathematical line. For a rapid decision, we must use only integer arithmetic and so we need an integer variable whose sign indicates which pixel to select. At $x_r + 1$,

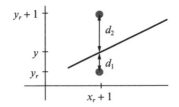

Figure 10.3 Vertical pixel separations from the mathematical line.

the vertical pixel separations from the mathematical line are labelled d_1 and d_2, as shown in Fig. 10.3.

The y coordinate on the mathematical line at $x_r + 1$ is calculated as

$$y = m(x_r + 1) + k$$

and so

$$d_1 = y - y_r = m(x_r + 1) + k - y_r$$
$$d_2 = (y_r + 1) - y = y_r + 1 - m(x_r + 1) - k$$

The difference between these two separations is

$$d_1 - d_2 = 2m(x_r + 1) - 2y_r - 2k - 1$$

Clearly, if $d_1 > d_2$ then $d_1 - d_2$ is positive and $(y_r + 1)$ is the nearer pixel and the one to be set. Programmatically, the determination of $d_1 - d_2$ requires floating point arithmetic. Bresenham showed how to compute a decision parameter p by rearranging the above equation so that it involves only integer calculations:

$$dx = x_1 - x_0$$
$$dy = y_1 - y_0$$
$$m = dy/dx$$
$$p_r = dx(d_1 - d_2) = 2x_r dy - 2y_r dx + 2dy + dx(2k - 1)$$

As dx is always positive in the first octant, the sign of p_r is the same as the sign of $d_1 - d_2$. If p_r is positive then both x and y are incremented, and the new value of p will be

$$p_{r+1} = 2(x_r + 1)dy - 2(y_r + 1)dx + 2dy + dx(2k - 1)$$

Otherwise only x is incremented and

```
#include "device.h"

void BresLineIncX (int xStart, int yStart, int xFinish, int yFinish)
{
    int dx = abs (xStart - xFinish), dy = abs (yStart - yFinish);
    int p = 2 * dy - dx; // Initialize p
    int TwiceDy = 2 * dy, TwiceDyLessDx = 2 * (dy - dx);
    int x, y, xEnd;

    // Determine if start and finish points should be interchanged
    if (xStart > xFinish) {
        x = xFinish;
        y = yFinish;
        xEnd = xStart;
    }
    else {
        x = xStart;
        y = yStart;
        xEnd = xFinish;
    {
    setPixel (x, y);            // Start point

    while (x < xEng)            {
        x++;                    // Increment x by 1
        if (p < 0)
            p += TwiceDy;       // p increment when only x is incremented
        else {
            y ++;
            p += TwiceDyLessDx; // p increment - x and y are incremented
        }
        setPixel (x, y);
    }
end;
```

Figure 10.4 C++ implementation of Bresenham's line algorithm.

$$p_{r+1} = 2(x_r + 1)dy - 2y_r dx + 2dy + dx(2k - 1)$$

In the first case,

$$p_{r+1} = p_r + 2(dy - dx)$$

and in the second case

$$p_{r+1} = p_r + 2dy$$

The C++ code (Fig. 10.4) is an implementation of Bresenham's algorithm for cases where $m \leq 1$. Notice that the first step is to determine if the start and finish points should be interchanged. Thereafter, parameter p is continuously updated to facilitate a rapid decision about which pixel to set next. It is assumed that the following pixel-setting function call is available: `setPixel (x, y)`.

10.3 Bresenham's circle algorithm

Bresenham developed this incremental circle generator for use in digital pen plotters. The algorithm generates all points on a circle centred at the origin by incrementing all the way around the circle. At each stage, there are two candidate pixels (as with the above line algorithm), and the selected pixel will have the smaller vertical or horizontal displacement from the mathematical arc. The procedure is perhaps best explained by examining a 45° arc of radius R in the second octant. It is in this octant that x is always incremented by one. The coordinate range is from $(0, R)$ to $(R/\sqrt{2}, R/\sqrt{2})$, as shown in Fig. 10.5.

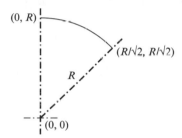

Figure 10.5 Arc in second octant.

The strategy is to select which of two pixels is closer to the circle by evaluating a function at the midpoint between the two pixels. In the second octant, if pixel P at (x_p, y_p) has been previously chosen as closest to the circle, the choice of the next pixel is between pixel S and pixel T, as shown in Fig. 10.6.

We define a function $F(x, y) = x^2 + y^2 - R^2$. This function is zero on the circle, positive outside the circle, and negative inside the circle. Notice that the midpoint between S and T is marked in Fig. 10.6. The coordinates of this midpoint are

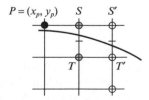

Figure 10.6 Choosing the pixel nearest to the arc segment.

$(x_p + 1, y_p - \frac{1}{2})$

and therefore function F has the value:

$(x_p + 1)^2 + (y_p - \frac{1}{2})^2 - R^2.$

It is clear from Fig. 10.6 that the midpoint between S and T lies inside the circle and hence function F would be negative and it would be logical to choose pixel S as the next one to be set. Function F can therefore be used as a decision parameter d. All that is now required for a working algorithm is a means of continuously updating d, using a minimum of arithmetic. If pixel S were chosen as the pixel to follow P, then the value of this decision parameter would be

$d = (x_p + 1)^2 + (y_p - \frac{1}{2})^2 - R^2$

Then, x would be incremented by 1 and it would be necessary to choose between pixels S' and T'. At the midpoint between them the decision variable would have the value

$d_{new} = (x_p + 2)^2 + (y_p - \frac{3}{2})^2 - R^2$

from which it may be shown that

$d_{new} = d + (2x_p - 2y_p + 5)$

Hence, the new decision variable can easily be computed from the previous one. Of course, it is necessary to compute the initial value. We round the radius R to the nearest integer and hence (for the second octant) the initial pixel lies on the circle at $(0, R)$. The next midpoint is at $(1, R - \frac{1}{2})$, so the initial value of d is

$1 + (R - \frac{1}{2})^2 - R^2 = \frac{5}{4} - R$

The problem with this decision variable is that it has to be computed using real arithmetic. To avoid this, we define a new decision variable $h = d - \frac{1}{4}$.

As the initial value of $d = \frac{5}{4} - R$, the initial value of h will be $1 - R$. As the initial value of h is an integer, and it is incremented by integer values, we still only need to test if

$h < 0$

to decide which pixel to set.

The following C code (Fig. 10.7) is an implementation of the algorithm for the second octant with the centre of the circle at the origin. It is easily extended for drawing a complete circle with its centre elsewhere: see Exercise 2 at the end of this chapter.

```
#include "device.h"

void BresArcOct2 (int Radius)
{
    int x = 0, y = Radius;      // start at 12 o'clock position
    int h = 1 - Radius;         // initialize decision variable

    setPixel (x, y);

    while (y > x) {
        if (h < 0) {
            h += 2 * x + 3;          // update when only x is incremented
            x++;
        }
        else {
            h += 2 * (x - y) + 5; // update when x and y are incremented
            x++;
            y--;
        }
        setPixel (x, y);
end;
```

Figure 10.7 C++ implementation of Bresenham's circle algorithm.

10.4 Filling algorithms

Many readers will be familiar with the 'paint bucket' tool that is part of the Microsoft Windows accessory.

Mspaint

The user chooses the colour required from a palette, selects the bucket tool from a set of tool icons and positions the cursor inside the region to be filled, as shown in Fig. 10.8(a). As soon as the mouse button is clicked, the selected region is filled with the chosen colour, as in Fig. 10.8(b).

Any algorithm that performs this type of operation is dubbed a 'fill' algorithm. We will look at two types of fill algorithms: the 'boundary fill' and the 'flood fill'. First, it is necessary to examine exactly what a region means, and to explain the term 'connectivity'. A region is a collection of pixels, and there are two basic types of region. A region is '4-connected' if any pair of pixels chosen at random is joined by a sequence of pixels by moving only horizontally or vertically. Figure 10.9 shows pixels that form a 4-connected region. Trace a path between any two, using the intermediate ones as stepping-stones, and you will see that it is never necessary to move diagonally.

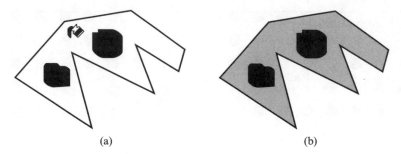

(a)   (b)

Figure 10.8 Selecting a region, and the result of the filling operation.

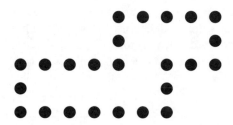

Figure 10.9 A 4-connected region.

Figure 10.10 An 8-connected region.

A region is 8-connected if any pair of pixels chosen at random can only be joined by moving diagonally, as well as horizontally and vertically. Figure 10.10 shows pixels that form an 8-connected region.

Clearly, every 4-connected region is also an 8-connected region, but the reverse is not true. A region can be defined in two ways. An 'interior-defined' region is the largest connected region, every pixel of which has colour C. A 'boundary-defined' region is the largest connected region, every pixel of which is *not* some boundary colour B.

It follows that every pixel of an interior-defined region is the same colour, but there may be different coloured pixels within a boundary-defined region, provided none of them has colour B. Figure 10.11 shows both types of region.

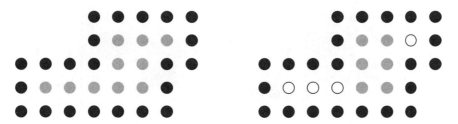

Figure 10.11 Interior-defined region (left) and boundary-defined region.

The pixels of the interior-defined region are all grey, whereas those of the boundary-defined region are white and grey.

Algorithms that fill interior-defined regions are called 'flood-fill' algorithms. Those that fill boundary-defined regions are called 'boundary-fill' algorithms. Notice that the Microsoft 'paint bucket' tool illustrated in Fig. 10.8 is evidently calling a flood-fill routine. If it were using a boundary-fill routine then the black blobs would also have become grey. We can conclude that the tool operates upon interior-defined regions.

A simple algorithm moves from the starting pixel in four directions and applies the algorithm recursively. If the colour of the interior-defined region is C and it is to be changed to D, then if the colour of the pixel with address (i, j) is C it is changed to D and the procedure calls itself for pixels with addresses $(i - 1, j)$, $(i + 1, j)$, $(i, j - 1)$, $(i, j + 1)$. If the colour of a pixel is not C then the procedure does nothing. Recursive procedures are relatively slow and can cause stack overflow when memory is limited. More efficient methods have been developed; typically they fill a horizontal 'span' of pixels across a scan-line. It is still necessary to stack unprocessed spans, but this is far better than stacking all unprocessed positions adjacent to the current position.

Starting from the initial interior point, we first fill in the contiguous span of pixels on this starting scan line. We then locate and stack starting positions for spans on the adjacent scan lines, where spans are defined as the contiguous horizontal string of positions bounded by pixels displayed in the region border colour. At each subsequent step we pop the next start position off the stack and repeat the process.

Figure 10.12 illustrates the above process for a boundary-defined region. The starting pixel is shown as an open circle. All the pixels in its span are changed to colour D at phase (a) and the spans on two adjacent scan lines are identified and pushed onto the stack. At phase (b) the top of the stack is popped and processed.

A new span (3) is identified and this is pushed onto the stack. At phase (c) span 3 is popped and processed. A new span (4) is identified and this is pushed onto the stack. At phase (d) span 4 is popped and processed. Two new spans (5 and 6) are identified and pushed onto the stack.

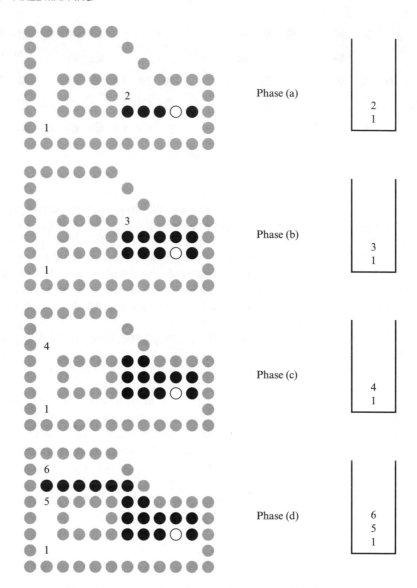

Figure 10.12 Scan-line filling of a boundary-defined region.

The rest of the filling process is not illustrated in Fig. 10.12, but it would proceed as follows. Span 6 is popped and processed. No new span can be identified and so span 5 is popped. Span 5 is a single pixel and a new span (7) would be identified below it and pushed onto the stack. One further single pixel span (8) would be identified, pushed onto the stack, popped immediately and processed. After span 8 has been processed no new span can be identified and so span 1 is popped – at last. No new span can be identified after span 1 is processed. The stack is now empty, and the filling operation is complete.

10.5 **Summary**

- The vast majority of contemporary graphics systems are pixel mapped, and so graphics constructs (such as lines and circles) have to be created by setting a group of pixels that approximates closely to the mathematical shape.
- Pixel mapping makes it possible to have text with many different fonts and sizes. A number of standard styles of text, such as *italic*, **bold** and underline (and combinations thereof), as well as superscript and subscript, are facilitated by pixel mapping.
- Pixel mapped entities can be scaled directly from the pixel map. However, scaling is better done starting with a vector representation of the entity, scaling that, and then doing the pixel mapping.
- Routines, such as Bresenham's line and circle algorithms, are implemented in *hardware*. This means that they are incorporated into the read only memory of the machine and run very much faster than a software implementation.
- Full details of two of Bresenham's algorithms have been given in this chapter because they are important in the history of computer graphics. They also demonstrate the important point that fast rendering can only be achieved when an algorithm has been devised that uses only integer arithmetic.
- Filling algorithms operate upon 'boundary-defined' and 'interior-defined' areas. Algorithms that fill interior-defined regions are called 'flood-fill' algorithms and are, perhaps, the most commonly found and widely used.
- The implementation of flood-fill algorithms is in hardware. The filling algorithm described in this chapter is an important example of the 'divide and conquer' paradigm, executed by using a 'last in – first out' stack.

10.6 **Further reading**

Bresenham, J. E., 'Algorithm for Computer Control of a Digital Plotter', *IBM Systems Journal*, Vol. 4, No. 1, pp. 25–30, 1965.

Bresenham, J. E., 'A Linear Algorithm for Incremental Digital Display of Circular Arcs', *Communications of the ACM*, Vol. 20, No. 2 February, pp. 100–106, 1977.

Firebaugh, M. W., *Computer Graphics. Tools for Visualization*, Wm. C. Brown Publishers, Dubuque, 1993.

Fishkin, K. P., and B. A. Barsky, 'A Family of New Algorithms for Soft Filling', *SIGGRAPH 84*, pp. 235–244, 1984.

Levoy, M., 'Area Flooding Algorithms', *Two-Dimensional Computer Animation, SIGGRAPH 82*, Course Notes 9, 1982. Levoy developed another enhancement that speeded up the process.

Lieberman, H., 'How to Color in a Coloring Book', *SIGGRAPH 87*, pp. 111–118, 1987. Lots of practical details.

Pavlidis, T. 'Contour Filling in Raster Graphics', *CGIP*, Vol. 10, No. 2, pp. 126–141, 1979.

Smith, A. R., 'Tint Fill', *SIGGRAPH 79*, pp. 276–283, 1979. Smith improved earlier algorithms by avoiding redundant examinations of adjacent scan lines.

Exercises

1. Adapt the C++ code given in Fig. 10.4 to demonstrate how a pixel-mapped line is generated. The demonstration program should prompt the user to input the coordinates of the start and finish points of the line. The line should then be drawn as a series of filled in circles (like the one shown in Fig. 10.2) in order to show clearly how the line is constructed.

2. Adapt the C++ code given in Fig. 10.7 to draw a complete circle whose radius and centre are input by the program user. As with Exercise 1, the pixels should be indicated by filled in circles.

3. Adapt the program that you wrote for Exercise 1, so that it displays a pixel-mapped rectangle whose width and height are specified by the user.

4. Adapt the program that you wrote for Exercise 3, so that it displays a pixel-mapped rectangle with rounded corners. Each corner will become a 90° arc whose radius is specified by the user. It will be necessary to check that the radius is not excessive.

5. How would you select the pixels that best approximate to the curve $y = x^2$, using only integer arithmetic?

6. See how many graphics packages you can discover that have a filling tool. How many such tools are boundary-fill, and how many are flood-fill?

7. Write a program to carry out the scan-line filling process illustrated in Fig. 10.12. Hint: you may find it helpful to develop a prototype program using a spreadsheet.

CHAPTER 11

High realism

11.1 **Introduction**

Perhaps the most obvious and desirable application of computer graphics is to generate an image that is so realistic that only an expert can distinguish between it and a photograph of the scene that it represents. A professional photographer has to recover the costs of premises and equipment, the hire of both models and locations, and travel expenses. The photographer naturally expects to make a good income from what is left when expenses are paid. Therefore, it was argued, as computer graphics becomes cheaper and more powerful, and photography more expensive, there must be a break-even point when the computer solution is the economic one.

Let us look first at some of the features that may be observed in a real scene.

- All the colours that the human eye can see.
- Natural and artificial lighting.
- Some of the objects in the scene reflect light and some refract it. There may be some objects that do both. Some objects may be visible through others that are transparent, or semi-transparent.
- Depending upon the nature of the lighting, objects may cast shadows. Within a shadow, the intensity of the light reflected from the shadowed object is reduced.
- It is rare for even a manufactured object to have a perfectly smooth surface. Most surfaces have some grain or texture. Natural objects have a very complex surface texture. Very few surfaces are flat, and so the intensity of light reflected from them towards the viewer is varying in a complex manner.
- Movement.

The list is somewhat daunting, but by the 1980s hardware and software had been developed that could produce very good quality still pictures from object representations that used both Euclidean geometry and fractals. At that stage, the cost was horrendous. As a result of demand from creative artists, as well as from purely representational image-makers, prices have fallen significantly and the capabilities of hardware/software systems have markedly improved.

There is now a real choice to be made between photography and computer-generated images. Moreover, creative artists now have an exciting, affordable new medium in which to work. Clearly, the scope of this topic is vast, so we will examine just a few of the fundamental problems in this chapter.

11.2 **True perspective**

In Chapter 6, we examined the quantitative effect of rotating a geometric model around the three axes. It was pointed out that one very useful series of rotations of this kind could be used to create an 'isometric' view of a solid object, like Fig. 9.13 on page 124. The `IsoView` procedure listed in Chapter 6 is a convenient and computationally cheap method for giving the viewer an impression of the solid object. Nevertheless, an isometric view is not a correct rendering of what a viewer sees. The rotation of the object is mathematically correct, but the rendering is then flawed by projecting parallel rays from all features of the object on to the viewport, with the result shown in Fig. 11.1a.

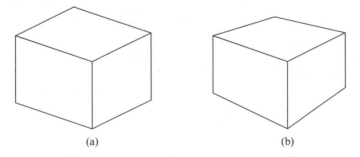

(a)   (b)

Figure 11.1 Isometric and perspective views of a cuboid.

As the projection is parallel, anyone looking at the 3D shape gets no cues as to how far away a feature of the object is from the viewer's eyes. The viewer will see a cuboid as three parallelograms with parallel edges remaining parallel, as in Fig. 11.1a. Instead, the parallel edges of the cube should appear to converge to three distant points known as vanishing points, as in Fig. 11.1b. The rate at which the edges appear to converge indicates to the viewer the depth of certain features. Conversely, the nearer the vanishing point, the closer the viewer perceives himself to be to the object.

The isometric view with its parallel edges can give the curious impression that its rear is larger than its front. This is because the human eye–brain system is accustomed to parallel lines having a vanishing point, and so lines that are actually parallel are perceived as divergent.

Fortunately, the geometry of true perspective is not complex. We will not consider stereoscopic vision, so the one eyeball of the viewer is at $z = Z_{view}$. A point $P = (x, y, z)$ within the image being viewed is therefore at a horizontal distance of $Z_{view} - z$ from the viewer. If the screen is at Z_{screen}, then the distance

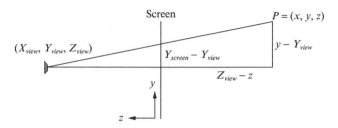

Figure 11.2 Scaling down for perspective effect.

from point P to screen is $Z_{screen} - z$ and values of x and y need to be scaled down in the ratio $(Z_{view} - Z_{screen})/(Z_{view} - z)$. The geometry is shown in Fig. 11.2.
Because triangles are similar:

$$\frac{Y_{screen} - Y_{view}}{y - Y_{view}} = \frac{Z_{view} - Z_{screen}}{Z_{view} - z}$$

and hence

$$Y_{screen} = Y_{view} + \frac{(Z_{view} - Z_{screen})(y - Y_{view})}{Z_{view} - z}$$

The same scaling applies to X_{screen} and so:

$$X_{screen} = X_{view} + \frac{(Z_{view} - Z_{screen})(x - X_{view})}{Z_{view} - z}$$

The equations are simplified if the viewer is considered to be at $(0, 0, Z_{view})$, i.e. at the centre of the screen. The scaling equations then become:

$$X_{screen} = \frac{(Z_{view} - Z_{screen})x}{Z_{view} - z} \quad \text{and} \quad Y_{screen} = \frac{(Z_{view} - Z_{screen})y}{Z_{view} - z}$$

The x and y object dimensions are scaled down in the ratio

$$\frac{\text{distance from viewer to screen}}{\text{distance from viewer to object}}$$

11.3 Ray casting

In ray casting, a ray is sent out from each screen pixel position to locate points on the surface of the object or scene. This makes it possible to decide whether

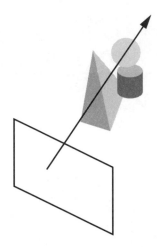

Figure 11.3 One ray cast from a pixel position.

or not a monochrome pixel is set, or the value on a grey scale to give to that pixel. One of the original reasons for writing ray-casting software was the search for yet another solution to the visible surface problem. The technique is quite useful when dealing with a group of objects (a scene) when a surface is visible only if it is the surface that is nearest to the screen shown in Fig. 11.3.

The single ray that is shown appears to intersect two surfaces of the pyramid and then pass through the sphere. It misses the cylinder altogether. Hence, the distances from the screen to the intersected surfaces are computed, and the pixel is set to the colour of the surface nearest the screen.

11.4 **Ray tracing**

Ray tracing is an extension of ray casting. Instead of simply looking for the *visible surface* for each pixel, we continue (mathematically) to reflect and refract the ray around the scene, collecting intensity contributions. This is illustrated in Fig. 11.4.

After being reflected by the pyramid (surface S_1), the reflected ray R_1 then strikes a transparent cylinder (surface S_2). Some of the ray T_1 is then refracted (transmitted), passes through the cylinder, is refracted again when it emerges from the cylinder, and finally stops at the natural light source shown conventionally. The other part of the ray striking the cylinder (R_2) is reflected and goes on to terminate at the artificial source of light that is shown.

The algorithm provides a simple and powerful technique for obtaining global reflection and refraction effects. The basic ray-tracing algorithm also provides for visible surface detection, shadow effects, transparency, and multiple light-source

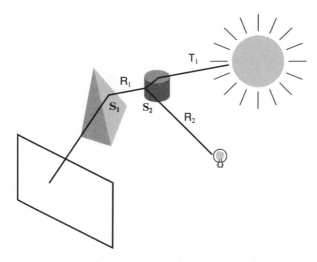

Figure 11.4 Tracing a ray back to sources of light.

illumination. Enhancements to the basic algorithm have been developed to produce photo-realistic displays. Ray-traced displays can be highly realistic, especially for shiny objects, but they are computationally expensive.

We first set up a coordinate system with the pixel positions designated in the *xy* plane. The scene description is given in this reference frame. From the centre of projection, we then determine a ray path that passes through the centre of each screen-pixel position. Illumination effects accumulated along this ray path are then assigned to the pixel. This rendering approach is based on the principles of geometric optics. Light rays from the surfaces in a scene emanate in all directions, and some will pass through the pixel positions in the projection plane.

Since there is an infinite number of ray paths, we determine the contributions to a particular pixel by tracing a light path *backwards* from the pixel to the scene. We consider the basic ray-tracing algorithm with one ray per pixel, which is equivalent to viewing the scene through a pinhole camera.

For each pixel ray, we test each surface in the scene to determine if the ray intersects it. If a surface is intersected, we calculate the distance from the pixel to the surface intersection point. The smallest such distance identifies the visible surface for that pixel. We then reflect the ray off the visible surface along a specular path (angle of reflection equals angle of incidence). If the surface is transparent, we also send a ray through the surface in the refraction direction. Reflection and refraction rays are referred to as 'secondary rays'.

This procedure is repeated for each secondary ray: objects are tested for intersection, and the nearest surface along a secondary ray path is used to recursively produce the next generation of reflection and refraction paths. As the rays from a pixel ricochet through the scene, each successively intersected surface is added to a binary ray-tracing tree. We use left branches in the tree to represent

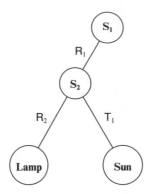

Figure 11.5 Binary ray-tracing tree for Fig. 11.4.

reflection paths, and the right branches represent transmission paths. Maximum depth of the ray-tracing trees can be set as a user option, or it can be determined by the amount of storage available. A path in the tree is then terminated if it reaches the pre-set maximum or if the ray strikes a light source.

The ray-tracing tree shown in Fig. 11.5 describes the situation illustrated in Fig. 11.4.

The intensity assigned to a pixel is then determined by accumulating the intensity contributions, starting at the leaf nodes of its ray-tracing tree. Surface intensity from each node in the tree is attenuated by the distance from the parent surface – the next node up the tree – and added to the intensity of the parent surface. Pixel intensity is then the sum of the attenuated intensities at the root node of the ray tree. If a pixel ray intersects no surfaces, the ray-tracing tree is empty and the pixel is assigned the intensity of the background. If a pixel ray intersects a non-reflecting light source, the pixel can be assigned the intensity of the source, although light sources are usually placed beyond the path of the initial rays.

First, we consider some simple models for calculating light intensities. The following empirical models provide simple and fast methods for calculating surface intensity at a given point, and they produce reasonably good results for most scenes. Lighting calculations are based on the optical properties of surfaces, the background lighting conditions, and the light-source specifications. Optical parameters are used to set surface properties, such as glossy, matt, opaque, and transparent. This controls the amount of reflection and absorption of incident light. All light sources are considered to be point sources, specified with a coordinate position and an intensity value (colour).

A surface that is not exposed directly to a light source will still be visible if nearby objects are illuminated. In our basic illumination model, we can set a general level of brightness for a scene. This is a simple way to model the combination of light reflections from various surfaces to produce a uniform illumination called the 'ambient light'. Ambient light has no spatial or directional character-istics. The amount of ambient light incident on each object is a constant for all surfaces and over all directions.

We can set the level for the ambient light in a scene with a parameter Ψ, and each surface is then illuminated with this constant value. The resulting reflected light is a constant for each surface, independent of the viewing direction and the orientation of the surface. However, the *intensity* of the reflected light depends upon the optical properties of the surface. These properties determine how much of the incident energy is to be reflected and how much absorbed.

Ambient light reflection is an approximation of global diffuse lighting effects. Diffuse reflections are constant over each surface in a scene, independent of the viewing direction. The fractional amount of the incident light that is diffusely reflected can be set for each surface with parameter ρ, the diffuse-reflection coefficient. Parameter ρ is assigned a constant value in the range 0.0–1.0, according to the reflecting properties we want the surface to have. If we want a highly reflective surface, we set the value of ρ near 1.0. This produces a bright surface with the intensity of the reflected light near that of the incident light.

To simulate a surface that absorbs most of the incident light, we set the reflectivity to a value near 0.0. In fact, the diffuse reflectivity is a function of surface colour, but we will assume that it is simply a constant for a particular surface.

If a surface is exposed only to ambient light, we can express the intensity of the diffuse reflection at any point on the surface as

$$D = \rho \Psi$$

Since ambient light produces a flat uninteresting shading for each surface, scenes are rarely rendered with ambient light alone. At least one light source is included in a scene, often as a point source at the viewing position.

We can model the diffuse reflections of illumination from a point source in a similar way. That is, we assume that the diffuse reflections from the surface are scattered with equal intensity in all directions, independent of the viewing direction. Such surfaces are sometimes referred to as 'ideal diffuse reflectors'. They are also called 'Lambertian reflectors', since radiated light energy from any point on the surface is governed by Lambert's cosine law. This law states that the radiant energy from any small surface area dA in any direction ϕ_N relative to the surface normal is proportional to $\cos \phi_N$ The light intensity depends upon the radiant energy per projected area perpendicular to direction ϕ_N, which is $dA \cos \phi_N$. Hence, for Lambertian reflection, the intensity of light is the same over all viewing directions.

Even though there is equal light scattering in all directions from a perfect diffuse reflector, the apparent brightness of the surface does depend upon the orientation of the surface relative to the light source. A surface that is oriented perpendicular to the direction of the incident light appears brighter than if the

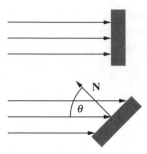

Figure 11.6 Brightness varies with angle between rays and surface.

surface were tilted at an oblique angle to the direction of the incoming light. This is easily seen by holding a white sheet of card parallel to a nearby window and slowly rotating the sheet away from the window direction. As the angle between the surface normal and the incoming light direction increases, less of the incident light falls on the surface, as shown in Fig. 11.6.

A beam of light rays is incident upon two surface patches of equal area, but with different orientations relative to the incident light direction. The angle of incidence between the incoming light direction and the surface normal is θ and so the projected area of a surface patch perpendicular to the light direction is proportional to $\cos\theta$. Hence, the intensity of illumination depends upon $\cos\theta$. If the incoming light from the source is perpendicular to the surface at a particular point, that point is fully illuminated.

As the angle of illumination moves away from the surface normal, the brightness of the point drops off. If Ψ_P is the intensity of the point light source, then the diffuse reflection equation for a point on the surface can be written as:

$$D_P = \rho \Psi_P \cos \theta$$

A surface is illuminated by a point source only if the angle of incidence is in the range 0°–90° and hence its cosine is in the range 0–1. When $\cos\theta$ is negative, the light source is behind the surface.

If N is the unit normal vector to a surface and S is the unit direction vector to the point light source from a point on the surface (Fig. 11.7) then $\cos\theta = N \cdot S$ and the diffuse refection equation for single point source illumination is

$$D_P = \rho \Psi_P (N \cdot S)$$

Figure 11.7 shows a surface intersected by a ray and the unit vectors needed for the reflected light-intensity computations.

Unit vector I is in the direction of the ray path. N is the unit surface normal. R is the unit reflection vector. S is the unit vector pointing to the light

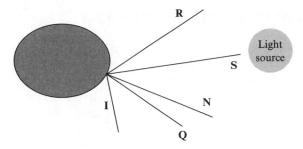

Figure 11.7 Unit vectors for light intensity computations.

source. **Q** is the unit vector whose direction bisects the angle between **S** and − **I**. The path along **S** is referred to as the 'shadow ray'. If any object intersects the shadow ray between the surface and the point light source, the surface is in shadow with respect to that source. The direction of the secondary ray path depends upon the surface normal and the incoming ray direction.

For a transparent surface, we also need to obtain intensity contributions from light transmitted through the material. We can locate the source of this contribution by tracing a secondary ray along the transmission direction. The unit transmission vector can be obtained from vectors **I** and **N**. Of course, it is also affected by the indices of refraction of the incident material and the refracting material. The various parameters are shown in Fig. 11.8.

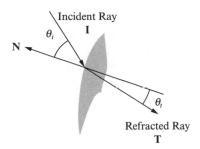

Figure 11.8 The geometry of refraction.

Snell's law provides the relationship between these parameters:

θ_i is the angle between the incident ray and the unit surface normal
θ_t is the angle between the refracted ray and the unit surface normal
η_i is the index of refraction in the incident material
η_t is the index of refraction in the refracting material

$$\cos\theta_t = \sqrt{1 - (\eta_i/\eta_t)^2(1 - \cos^2\theta_i)}$$

11.5 **Polygon rendering techniques**

We now turn our attention to the application of an illumination model to the rendering of standard graphics objects – those formed with polygon surfaces. The objects are usually polygon-mesh approximations of curved surface objects, but they can also be polyhedra that are not curved-surface approximations. Scan-line algorithms typically apply a lighting model to obtain polygon surface rendering in one of two ways. Each polygon can be rendered with a single intensity, or the intensity can be obtained at each point of the surface using an interpolation scheme.

11.5.1 *Constant-intensity shading*

A fast and simple method for rendering an object with polygon surfaces is constant-intensity shading, also known as 'flat shading'. In this method, a single intensity is calculated for each polygon. All points over the surface of the polygon are then displayed with the same intensity value. Constant shading can be useful for quickly displaying the general appearance of a curved surface. The cone illustrated in Fig. 11.9 comprises a large number of isosceles triangles. Any particular triangle has the same flat shading, and the intensity is only slightly different from the adjacent triangles. The effect is that the edges of the triangles (facets) are obvious to the viewer, who nevertheless gets some impression of an illuminated curved surface.

Flat shading is generally considered to provide an accurate rendering for an object if all of the following conditions apply:

- The object is a polyhedron and is not an approximation of an object with a curved surface.
- All light sources illuminating the object are sufficiently far from the surface so that $\cos \theta = \mathbf{N} \cdot \mathbf{S}$ and the attenuation function are constant over the surface.

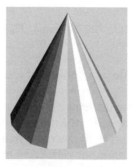

Figure 11.9 Constant-intensity shading.

- The viewing position is sufficiently far from the surface so that $\mathbf{V} \cdot \mathbf{R}$ is constant over the surface.

11.5.2 *Gouraud shading*

This intensity-interpolation scheme, developed by Gouraud and generally referred to as 'Gouraud shading', renders a polygon surface by linearly interpolating intensity values across the surface. Intensity values for each polygon are matched with the values of adjacent polygons along the common edges, thus eliminating the intensity discontinuities that can occur in flat shading.

Each polygon surface is rendered with Gouraud shading by performing the following calculations:

- determine the average unit normal vector at each polygon vertex,
- apply an illumination model to each vertex to calculate the vertex intensity,
- linearly interpolate the vertex intensities over the surface of the polygon.

At each polygon vertex, we obtain a normal vector by averaging the surface normals of all polygons sharing that vertex, as illustrated in Fig. 11.10. Thus, for any vertex position $\mathbf{V}$, we obtain the unit vertex normal with the calculation:

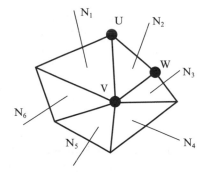

Figure 11.10 Six polygons that share vertex **V**.

$$N_{\mathbf{v}} = \frac{\sum\limits_{k=1}^{n} N_k}{\left| \sum\limits_{k=1}^{n} N_k \right|}$$

Once we have the vertex normals, we can determine the intensity at the vertices from a lighting model.

Figure 11.11 demonstrates the next step: interpolating intensities along the polygon edges. For each scan line, the intensity at the intersection of the scan line with a polygon edge is linearly interpolated from the intensities at the edge

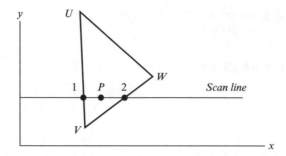

Figure 11.11 Linear interpolation for intensity at any point in triangle *UVW*.

end-points. For Fig. 11.11, the polygon edge with end-point vertices at positions U and V is intersected by the scan line at point 1. A fast method for obtaining the intensity at point 1 is to interpolate between intensities I_U and I_V using only the vertical displacement of the scan line:

$$I_1 = \frac{y_1 - y_V}{y_U - y_V} I_U + \frac{y_U - y_1}{y_U - y_V} I_2$$

Similarly, intensity at the right intersection of this scan line (point 2) is interpolated from intensity values at vertices V and W. Once these bounding intensities are established for a scan line, an interior point (such as point P in Fig. 11.11) is interpolated from the bounding intensities at points 1 and 2 as

$$I_P = \frac{x_2 - x_P}{x_2 - x_1} I_1 + \frac{x_P - x_1}{x_2 - x_1} I_2$$

Incremental calculations are used to obtain successive edge intensity values between scan lines and to obtain successive intensities along a scan line. As shown in Fig. 11.12, if the intensity at edge position (x, y) is interpolated as

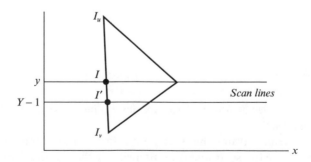

Figure 11.12 Linear interpolation between successive scan lines.

$$I = \frac{y - y_V}{y_U - y_V} I_U + \frac{y_U - y}{y_U - y_V} I_V$$

then we can obtain the intensity along this edge for the next scan line, $y - 1$, as

$$I' = I + \frac{I_V - I_U}{y_V - y_U}$$

Similar calculations are used to obtain intensities at successive horizontal pixel positions along each scan line. When surfaces are to be rendered in colour, the intensity of each colour component is calculated at the vertices. Gouraud shading can be combined with a visible surface algorithm to fill in the visible polygons along each scan line.

Gouraud shading removes the intensity discontinuities associated with the constant-shading model, but it has some other deficiencies. Highlights on the surface are sometimes displayed with anomalous shapes, and the linear intensity interpolation can cause bright or dark intensity streaks, called Mach bands, to appear on the surface. These effects can be reduced by dividing the surface into a greater number of polygon faces, or by using other methods, such as Phong shading, that require more calculations.

11.5.3 *Phong shading*

A more accurate method for rendering a polygon surface is to interpolate normal vectors, and then apply the illumination model to *each surface point*. This method, developed by Phong Bui Tuong, is called 'Phong shading', or 'normal-vector interpolation shading'. It displays more realistic highlights on a surface and greatly reduces the Mach-band effect.

A polygon surface is rendered using Phong shading by carrying out the following steps:

- determine the average unit normal vector at each polygon vertex,
- linearly interpolate the vertex normals over the surface of the polygon,
- apply an illumination model along each scan line to calculate projected pixel intensities for the surface points.

Interpolation of surface normals along a polygon edge between two vertices is illustrated in Fig. 11.13. The normal vector $\mathbf{N}$ for the scan-line intersection point along the edge between vertices U and V can be obtained by vertically interpolating between edge endpoint normals:

$$\mathbf{N} = \frac{y - y_V}{y_U - y_V} N_U + \frac{y_U - y}{y_U - y_V} N_V$$

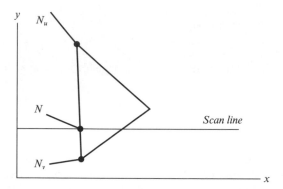

Figure 11.13 Interpolation of surface normals along a polygon edge.

Incremental methods are used to evaluate normals between scan lines and along each individual scan line. At each pixel position along a scan line, the illumination model is applied to determine the surface intensity at that point.

Intensity calculations using an approximated normal vector at each point along the scan line produce more accurate results than the direct interpolation of intensities, as in Gouraud shading. The trade-off, however, is that Phong shading requires considerably more processor time.

11.6 **Texture**

11.6.1 *The nature of a real surface*

Both Gouraud and Phong shading are methods of rendering a perfectly smooth surface. The surface is assumed to be described precisely by its equations, and hence the coordinates of a point on the surface satisfy these equations. Of course, in practice, few such surfaces exist, and those that approximate to such perfection (e.g. the mirror of a reflecting telescope) can only be manufactured at great expense. The vast majority of surfaces have some irregularities, or some patterning. This is true of both natural objects and manufactured materials. In order to achieve high realism in the rendering of an image it is essential to be able to give all surfaces the appearance of the texture of the material of which they are composed.

A simple method for adding surface details is to model structure and patterns with polygon facets. For large-scale detail, polygon modelling can give good results. Some examples of such large-scale details are squares on a chess board, dividing lines on a highway, tile patterns on vinyl flooring, floral designs on a pile carpet, and panels on a door. An irregular surface can be modelled with small, randomly oriented polygon facets.

Surface-pattern polygons are generally overlaid on a larger surface polygon and are processed with the parent surface. Only the parent polygon is processed

 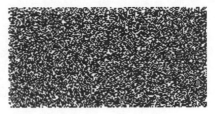

Figure 11.14 Displacement of up to four units (left), ten units (right).

by the visible surface algorithms, but the illumination parameters for the surface detail polygons take precedence over the parent polygon. When intricate or fine surface detail is to be modelled, polygon methods are not practicable. For example, it would be difficult to model the surface structure of a prune with polygon facets.

A very simple algorithm can be written that uses a random number generator to draw two diagonally adjacent pixels. Each pair of pixels is randomly displaced by up to a set number of pixel positions from the base scan line. The effects are illustrated in Fig. 11.14.

The objection to this technique is that the surface merely looks 'rough'; it does not look like any specific natural or manufactured surface, although the one on the right (if coloured green) might do for a lawn.

11.6.2 *Texture mapping*

A common method for adding surface details is to map texture patterns onto the surfaces of objects. The texture pattern may either be defined in a rectangular array or as a procedure that modifies surface intensity values. This approach is referred to as 'texture mapping' or 'pattern mapping'. Usually, the texture pattern is defined with a rectangular grid of intensity values in a texture space referenced with (s, t) coordinate values, as shown in Fig. 11.15.

Surface positions in the scene are referenced with uv object-space coordinates, and pixel position on the projection plane are referenced in xy cartesian coordinates.

Texture mapping can be accomplished in one of two ways:

a) map the texture pattern to object surfaces, then to the projection plane, or
b) map pixel areas onto object surfaces, then to texture space.

The former is often called 'texture scanning' and the latter is known as 'inverse scanning'.

To simplify calculations, the mapping from texture space to object space is specified with parametric linear functions

$$u = f_u(s, t) = a_u s + b_u t + c_u$$
$$v = f_v(s, t) = a_v s + b_v t + c_v$$

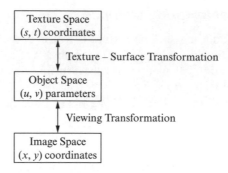

Figure 11.15 Coordinate reference systems.

The object-to-image space mapping is accomplished with the concatenation of the viewing and projection transformations. A disadvantage of mapping from texture space to pixel space is that a selected texture patch usually does not match up with the pixel boundaries, thus requiring calculation of the fractional area of pixel coverage. Therefore, mapping from image (pixel) space to texture space is the most commonly used texture-mapping method. This avoids pixel-subdivision calculations, and allows filtering procedures to be easily applied.

Figure 11.16 was produced by first mapping each pixel of the final image outline onto object space. In other words, the object coordinates of each pixel are established first. Next, the object coordinates are mapped onto texture space and the texture map specifies what is to happen to the pixel in question. The object is the same superquadric that is shown in Fig. 8.9. It was pointed out in Chapter 8 that the rendering of the superquadric was less than satisfactory because of the presence of Moiré fringes, and of surfaces that should be hidden. Now that the surface has a texture, and hidden surfaces are correctly hidden, it begins to look something like a solid object.

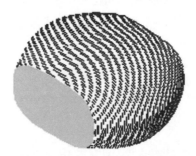

Figure 11.16 Texture applied to superquadric surface.

11.6.3 *Procedural texturing methods*

Another method for adding surface texture is to use procedural definitions of the colour variations that are to be applied to the objects of a scene. This approach avoids the transformation calculations involved in transferring two-dimensional texture patterns to object surfaces.

When values are assigned throughout a region of three-dimensional space, the object colour variations are dubbed 'solid textures'. Values from texture space are transferred to object surfaces using procedural methods, since it is usually impossible to store texture values for all points throughout a region of space. Other procedural methods can be used to set up texture values over 2-dimensional objects, such as bricks, to be rendered with the same texturing as the outside surfaces.

As examples of procedural texturing, wood grains or marble patterns can be created using sine curves defined in 3-dimensional space. Random variations in the wood or marble texturing can be attained by superimposing a noise function on the harmonic variations.

11.6.4 *Bump mapping*

Although texture mapping can be used to add fine surface details, it is not a good method for modelling the surface roughness that appears on fruits such as oranges and strawberries. The illumination detail in the texture pattern usually does not correspond to the illumination direction in the scene. A better method for creating surface bumpiness is to apply a perturbation function to the surface normal and then use the perturbed normal in the illumination model calculations. This technique is called 'bump mapping'.

If $P(u, v)$ represents a position on a parametric surface, we can obtain the surface normal at that point with the calculation

$$\mathbf{N} = \mathbf{P}_u \times \mathbf{P}_v$$

$\mathbf{P}_u$ and $\mathbf{P}_v$ are the partial derivatives of P with respect to parameters u and v. To obtain a perturbed normal, we modify the surface-position vector by adding a small perturbation function, called a bump function:

$$\mathbf{P}'(u, v) = \mathbf{P}(u, v) + b(u, v)\mathbf{n}$$

This adds bumps to the surface in the direction of the unit surface normal. The perturbed surface normal is then obtained as

$$\mathbf{N}' = \mathbf{P}'_u \times \mathbf{P}'_v$$

We calculate the partial derivative with respect to u of the perturbed position vector as

$$\mathbf{P}'_u = \frac{\partial}{\partial u}(\mathbf{P} + b\mathbf{n})$$

$$= \mathbf{P}_u + b_u\mathbf{n} + b\mathbf{n}_v$$

Assuming the bump function is small, we can neglect the last term and write:

$$\mathbf{P}'_u \approx \mathbf{P}_u + b_v\mathbf{n}$$

Similarly,

$$\mathbf{P}'_v \approx \mathbf{P}_v + b_v\mathbf{n}$$

11.7 Shadows and reflections

Visible surface methods (such as the scan line algorithm described in Chapter 9) can be used to locate areas where light sources produce shadows. By applying a visible surface method *with a light source at the viewing position*, we can determine which surface sections cannot be 'seen' from the light source. These are the shadow areas. For example, Fig. 9.13 (page 124) shows the 'stepped wedge' with Surface No. 5 partially visible. If the light were coming from the viewing position, then the hidden part of Surface No. 5 would be in shadow.

Once we have determined the shadow areas for all the light sources, the shadows could be treated as surface patterns and stored in pattern arrays. Figure 11.17 illustrates the generation of shading patterns for a cylinder and a cuboid standing on a horizontal plane with parallel rays of light coming from the direction indicated. All shadow areas in this figure are surfaces that are not visible from the position of the light source.

Shadow patterns generated by a visible surface method are valid for any selected viewing position, as long as the light-source positions are not changed. Surfaces that are visible from the view position are shaded according to the lighting model, which can be combined with texture patterns. We can display

Figure 11.17 Shadows are areas not visible from the light-source.

Figure 11.18 Reflections from and shadows on a textured surface.

shadow areas with ambient-light intensity only, or we can combine the ambient light with specified surface textures.

Figure 11.4 shows a situation where neither of the light sources is reflected directly towards the viewer. The sun's rays are refracted by the cylinder, and then they are reflected by the tetrahedron. Light from the lamp is reflected by the cylinder, then by the tetrahedron, before reaching the viewer. A 'highlight' should appear on the computer-generated image whenever it is theoretically possible for the viewer to see an image (however distorted and diffused) of a light source.

In flash photography, highlights can be something of a nuisance. Reflections from eyes, spectacle lenses and shiny skin are distracting and make it apparent to the experienced observer that the photograph was taken with a sudden burst of intense light. In order to get realistic highlights, like the model of a moonlit castle shown in Fig. 11.18, it is necessary to carry out the full ray-tracing operation that is described above. Notice that the highlights (on the circular turrets) are subtly emphasised by the shadows immediately below them. The texture of the stonework is readily apparent in the shadows, but less so where the same type of surface is reflecting light directly towards the viewer.

11.8 Summary

- True perspective projection is essential for realistic images. If parallel lines do not have a 'vanishing point' then they give the human eye–brain system the impression of divergence, which is at best distracting, and at worst irritating. The computational cost of perspective projection is not significantly greater than that of orthographic projection.

- Ray casting is the technique whereby an imaginary ray is sent from the eye of the viewer to each pixel position on the surface of the screen. The ray is followed until it meets the first solid surface within the scene that is modelled. This surface is what the viewer would be able to see, and hence ray casting may be classified as another method of solving the visible surface problem.

- The limitation of ray casting is that all that can be rendered is the texture of the surface that the viewer can see. Nothing is known about how the surface is illuminated, nor if any shadows are cast upon it. This information can be obtained by ray *tracing*, a procedure whereby each ray that is cast from eye to pixel position is traced onwards, as it is reflected or refracted by parts of the scene, until it either reaches a source of light or goes off to infinity. Rays that reach a source of light will have the corresponding pixel set according to the light source and the amount of reflection and refraction that has occurred.

- Constant-intensity shading can be applied to a facetted shape at very little computational expense. The facets will still be obvious to the viewer. This form of shading is acceptable if the object really is a polyhedron, if the light source is far away, and if the viewer is a long distance from the object.

- Gouraud shading renders a polygon surface by linearly interpolating intensity values across the surface. A curved surface that has been modelled with facets (patches, tiles) will not appear as a large number of small surfaces. Instead, the surfaces appear to blend smoothly and give the impression of a true curved surface. However, there are sometimes problems with distorted highlights and Mach bands.

- Phong shading displays more realistic highlights on a surface and greatly reduces the Mach-band effect. However, the computational cost of this method of shading is significantly more than Gouraud shading. For this reason, it is employed only when it is essential to have photographic quality images.

- Images do not look realistic if each surface is perfectly plain and smooth. A surface may be given a characteristic texture in several ways. Mapping from image (pixel) space to texture space is the most commonly used texture-mapping method. With such a technique, it is possible to give a surface roughness, or a grain (like wood), or a pattern (like bonded bricks).

- The texture-mapping method does not give good results for the irregular surfaces of fruits such as oranges and strawberries. Bump-mapping best renders such surfaces.

11.9 **Further reading**

For greater detail of the application of some of the mathematics presented in this chapter, the following are recommended.

Arvo, J. and D. Kirk, 'Fast Ray Tracing by Ray Classification', *Computer Graphics*, Vol. 21, No. 4, pp. 55–64, 1987.

Bishop, G. and D. M. Wiemer, 'Fast Phong Shading', *Computer Graphics*, Vol. 20, No. 4, pp. 103–106, 1986.

Blinn, J. F. and M. E. Newell, 'Texture and Reflection in Computer Generated Images', *CACM*, Vol. 19, No. 10, pp. 542–547, 1976.

Freeman, H. (Ed.), *Tutorial and Selected Readings in Interactive Computer Graphics*, IEEE Comp. Soc. Press, Silver Spring, Maryland, pp. 302–308, 1980. Edited version of Gouraud's paper in *IEEE Transactions on Computers*.

Hearn, D. and M. P. Baker, *Computer Graphics C Version*, Prentice Hall, Inc., Second Edition, 1997.

Gouraud, H., 'Continuous Shading of Curved Surfaces', *IEEE Transactions on Computers*, C-20(6), pp. 623–629, 1971.

Phong, B. T., 'Illumination for Computer-Generated Images', *CACM*, Vol. 18, No. 6, pp. 311–317, 1975.

Firebaugh, M. W., *Computer Graphics. Tools for Visualization*, Wm. C. Brown Publishers, Dubuque, 1993.

Newman, W. M. and R. F. Sproull, *Principles of Interactive Computer Graphics*, McGraw-Hill, New York, 1979.

Exercises

1. Write a program to draw a true perspective view of a cube. The user specifies the orientation of the cube, and his distance from it.
2. Enhance the program that you wrote for exercise 1 for stereoscopic vision. Project two separate, differently coloured images onto the screen, one for the left eye and one for the right eye. Human eyes are about 650 mm apart. If you are able to acquire or manufacture 3D spectacles, with appropriately coloured filters for each eye, test how well the stereoscopic effect works for you.
3. Use the B-rep model of the stepped wedge given in Fig. 9.3 to investigate the ray casting method. Rotate the stepped wedge so that it is in the position shown in Fig. 9.12, with Surface No. 5 partially visible. Cast rays from the viewer to the entire width of a scan line that intersects Surface No. 5. How does this technique compare in speed and accuracy with the scan line algorithm?
4. Introduce a source of light into a scene in which the only (opaque) object is the stepped wedge. Each surface of the object reflects and diffuses incident light. Trace rays from the viewer along one entire scan line to determine how a pixel should be set.

5. Add a cuboid to the scene described in exercise 4. Place the cuboid between the source of light and the stepped wedge so that it casts a shadow. Assume that the viewer is placed at the source of light, and hence determine the shape of the shadow cast by the cuboid. Select a scan line that includes some of the shadow, and determine how each pixel should now be set.

6. The superquadric illustrated in Fig. 8.9 has these defining equations:

$$x = a \sin \varphi \cos^{0.65} \theta \quad y = b \sin \varphi \sin^{0.65} \theta \quad z = 200\varphi$$

Figure 8.9 was produced by rotating the object through $-45°$ around the y axis and then rotating it through $\tan^{-1}(1/\sqrt{2})$ around the x axis. The constants are:

$$a = 160 \quad b = 100$$

Object coordinates (x, y) are pixel mapped as follows:

$$i = 400 + x \quad j = 100 - y$$

Compute the range of i and j values required to render the superquadric. In order to add texture to the surface, it is necessary to set up a procedure with nested loops, the outside loop for the range of i values, and the inner one for the range of j values. To invert the relationships between pixel space and object space, it will be necessary to set up an array that records the (θ, φ) coordinates that correspond to each pixel position.

Try out various texture spaces (s, t). A simple one to try first would be a rule that $s = \theta$, and a pixel is set only when s is exactly divisible by 0.03.

CHAPTER 12

Some advanced techniques

12.1 Introduction

In this final chapter, we examine several applications of computer graphics that not only exemplify the state of the art, but also indicate the enormous scope of this area of computer science. Some of the following applications, such as morphing, animation, and image enhancement are very firmly in the public gaze. This is because the uses to which they are put are frequently displayed on television, cinema and in print. Conversely, nesting applications are not of much public interest, but are very important in certain manufacturing industries. Charting falls into both categories: many applications are well known to the general public, whilst others are peculiar to certain professions, where they are of immense value.

Charting can be defined as 'the graphical presentation of data'. Hence, it covers such a wide range that it is necessary to narrow it down in order to eliminate several of the topics that have already been discussed. A geometric model is a set of data, and we have seen that such data have to be carefully structured, using validation principles, in order to be a true model. The graphical presentation of a geometric model is usually known as 'rendering' rather than 'charting'. We can arrive at a suitably narrower definition of charting if we exclude data that have been structured deliberately to model something with a physical form, and include only data that represent an abstract concept.

My annual expenditure pattern does not have a physical form, but I can indicate what percentage goes on energy, water, motoring, holidays, council tax, etc. in the form of a pie chart. Readers may be familiar with other ways of presenting statistical data, such as the bar chart, scatter chart, etc. For very little computational expense, such charts present the viewer with a helpful picture, and go some way to giving the data a meaning in human terms. There are other abstract concepts that are almost impossible to fathom unless they are presented graphically, and this is the area to be addressed in this chapter.

Family historians record what is technically known as 'lineage-linked' data. Everyone has two biological parents and in many societies parents and dependent children live together in family units. Such family units may include other persons related by blood or by law: for example fostered or adopted children, children from a previous marriage, grandparents, etc. Hence, families can be related to each other in a very complicated manner, which often cannot be comprehended until a suitable chart has been prepared. Another good example of data made meaningful in the form of a chart is the subject of project planning. The general principle of project planning is to start first on tasks that take the longest, in order to minimise delays. In industries as diverse as civil engineering, software development, film and theatre production, new projects are planned using scheduling software, and then charts are automatically generated for information and progress monitoring.

12.2 **Morphing**

Transformation of object shapes from one form to another is called 'morphing', which is a shortened form of 'metamorphosis'. Morphing methods can be applied to any motion or transition involving a change of shape. Given two 'key frames' for an object transformation, we first adjust the object specification in one of the frames so that the number of polygon edges (or the number of vertices) is the same for the two frames. The need for pre-processing is illustrated in Fig. 12.1. A straight-line segment in key frame k is transformed into two line segments in key frame $k + 1$. Since key frame $k + 1$ has an extra vertex, a vertex must be inserted between vertices A and B in key frame k to balance the number of vertices (and edges) in the two key frames.

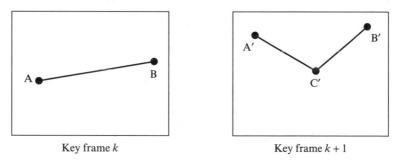

Key frame k Key frame $k + 1$

Figure 12.1 Consecutive key frames.

Using linear interpolation to generate the in-betweens, we transition the added vertex in key frame k into vertex C' along the straight-line path shown in Fig. 12.2.

For animation, there should be intermediate steps between key frame k and key frame $k + 1$. For example, the above shape could be the mouth of a cartoon face that is rising upwards. The mouth moves from scowl at key frame k to grin at key frame $k + 1$, with the two intermediate steps shown in Fig. 12.3. Vertex A at each intermediate step moves along vector AA' by an amount which is 33% of the length of the vector. A similar interpolation is carried out for vertices B and C.

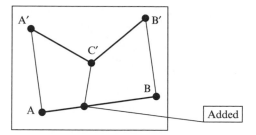

Figure 12.2 Linear interpolation for transition between key frames.

Key frame k Key frame $k + 1$

Figure 12.3 Morphing to change facial expression.

Morphing is frequently used in missing person enquiries to age a face when only an old photograph of the subject is available, and it is felt that it would be helpful to see how the face may have aged in the meantime. For example, the web site **www.missingkids.co.uk** (opened in March 2000) uses morphing to age the last available pictures of missing children. A skilful artist can take the photograph as the starting point, and use their experience to portray how the face would look at the present time. However, faces do not age at a fixed rate, and the subject may look either older or younger than the artist has predicted. When there is a witness who believes that they have seen the missing person, the digitised image can be morphed in steps as the witness watches, and tries to recognise the face that they have recently seen.

The line drawing in Fig. 12.4 is an idealised youthful male face, composed entirely of straight lines, which could have been digitised from a real photograph.

Figure 12.4 has a mere 250 lines, and this is an order of magnitude less than that required for reasonable accuracy in practice. However, it is far more typical of the morphing process than Fig. 12.1, because there is generally a very significant difference in the number of lines in successive key frames. In popular parlance, the human face is often said to become 'lined' as it ages, and this is precisely what happens in morphing. In general, the older the face, the more lines that are required for a realistic rendering.

Figure 12.4 Facial features as lines digitised from a photograph.

There are established formulae for equalising key frames in terms of either the number of lines or the number of vertices to be added to a key frame. It is often convenient to equalise the line count, and if

E_k =   number of lines in key frame k

E_{k+1} =   number of lines in key frame $k + 1$

then we define

E_{max} =   max (E_k, E_{k+1})

E_{min} =   min (E_k, E_{k+1})

From these we compute

N_a = E_{max} **mod** E_{min}

and

N_b = E_{max} **div** E_{min}

The pre-processing is accomplished by

1. dividing N_a lines of the key frame with the minimum number of lines into $N_b + 1$ parts,
2. dividing the remaining lines of this key frame into N_b parts.

Figure 12.5 Lines added and moved to age the face.

For example, suppose that the face has been aged as shown in Fig. 12.5. There are 250 edges in the first, and 320 edges in the second key frame.

Hence $E_{max} = 320$, $E_{min} = 250$, $N_a = 320$ **mod** $250 = 70$, $N_b = 320$ **div** $250 = 1$.

Therefore, it is necessary to divide 70 of the lines in key frame k (Fig. 12.4) into two sections, and the remaining edges of this key frame need no modification. The design of an algorithm to decide which lines to divide into sections is not a trivial matter, and it is often convenient to leave the decision to the creative person who is using morphing software. The user identifies the same vertices in consecutive frames, and thus informs the software of where splitting is to be done.

Notice that the process is complicated by the fact that, as with the ageing face, it is not simply a case of adding an intermediate vertex between the ends of an existing line. Instead, it will be necessary to create lines of zero length (null lines) at one end of 70 of the lines in Fig. 12.4. As soon as the interpolation process begins, these null lines have to be severed from their parent line and they acquire a finite length. In practice, it is better to define these 70 lines in key frame k. The vertices of any contiguous set of lines (like those on the aged forehead) all have the same coordinates in key frame k, and the set of lines becomes a single point. During the transition to key frame $k + 1$, the coordinates are changed and the lines progressively lengthen. The artist/user is best placed to decide on how the lines 'grow' as a face ages.

Of course, morphing software is far more sophisticated than this brief introduction may suggest. To get a realistic image of a face, skin tones, hair colouring, shading, and an apparent source of light will be necessary. Hence morphing may be properly regarded as the process of generating a highly realistic image from a *dynamic* geometric model, rather than the static model of Chapter 11. This definition of morphing actually requires further refinement because the dynamics of the geometric model are *internal*. In other words, the position of the model in space is fixed, but the component parts of the model move relative to each other. Moreover, some components may be added or subtracted. If the model does not remain stationary, then the process of generating an image from the model is generally known as 'animation', and we will now examine some of the techniques involved.

12.3 Animation

Notice that the intermediate steps in Fig. 12.3 represent an *equal* increment along the locus of each vertex. In reality, this is not what happens because of Newton's second law: 'every body continues in its state of rest, or uniform motion in a straight line, unless acted upon by a force'.

Of course, there will be occasions when the changes from one frame to the next occur at a uniform speed – zero acceleration. However, when a metamorphosis begins, it looks more acceptable if there is a uniform acceleration up to some uniform terminal speed. Similarly, at the end of the process there should be a uniform deceleration back to rest. In Fig. 12.3 the intermediate steps represent equal displacements in equal time. More natural effects can be achieved by using the equation below in which

t = time elapsed x = distance travelled in time t
v = initial speed a = constant acceleration

$$x = vt + at^2/2.$$

There are two classes of animation that need to be considered.

- Inanimate mechanisms. A mechanism is a set of components connected together in such a way that, if the position of one moving part is specified, then the positions of all the other moving parts may be computed.
- Living creatures. The limb movements of living creatures are not mechanistic. For example, if you place the tip of a forefinger on this graphics symbol ☺ then there is a wide range of possible positions for your finger joints, wrist, lower arm, upper arm, etc.

12.3.1 *Mechanisms*

We will look first at how to display the motion of a mechanism. The components of a mechanism can move relative to each other and the commonest types of movement are translation (sliding) and rotation. The technical name of the mechanism of the internal combustion engine is the 'slider-crank chain'. It is shown diagramatically in Fig. 12.6. It has one pair of components (piston and cylinder wall) whose relative motion is translation, and three pairs whose relative motion is rotational.

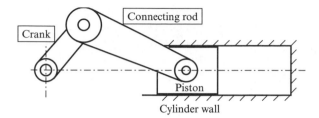

Figure 12.6 The slider-crank chain mechanism.

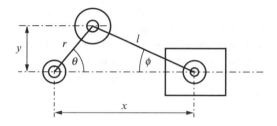

Figure 12.7 Geometry of the slider-crank chain mechanism.

Of course, the internal combustion engine also has inlet and exhaust valves that are operated by a camshaft, that is driven by the crankshaft. A complete animation would include the opening and closing of these valves, and show the fuel/air mixture entering, being compressed, ignited and exhausted. However, the general principles of mechanism animation can be examined just by treating the geometry of the slider-crank chain.

The fundamental geometry is shown in Fig. 12.7. The effective radius of the crank is a fixed distance r. The fixed distance between the connecting rod bearing centres is l. The variable angle between the crank and a line from the centre of the crank shaft through the centre of the cylinder is θ. As we are analysing a mechanism, we know that there will be an exact relationship between θ and the variable distance x between the centre of the crankshaft and the centre of the pin by which the connecting rod is attached to the cylinder. This relationship is readily established if we give a symbol ϕ to the angle between the connecting rod and the locus of the piston.

One other symbol is useful in the analysis: y is the vertical distance from the locus of the piston to the 'big end' of the connecting rod. We can now use trigonometry to set up an equation for x:

$$x = r \cos \theta + l \cos \phi$$

and eliminate ϕ from the above equation by noting that

$$y = r \sin \theta = l \sin \phi$$

Whence

$$\sin \phi = \frac{r}{l} \sin \theta$$

$$\cos \phi = \sqrt{1 - r^2 \sin^2 \theta / l^2}$$

$$x = r \cos \theta + \sqrt{l^2 - r^2 \sin^2 \theta}$$

We can now animate the slider-crank chain by starting at $\theta = 0°$ (when $x = r + l$) and incrementing in suitable steps. Notice that, when $\theta = 180°$, $x = l - r$. Most modern processors would be perfectly capable of performing the necessary computations in real time, especially if only two lines (representing the crank radius and the connecting rod) are drawn for each value of θ. Real time animation gets more problematic if a realistic crank, connecting rod and piston are to be drawn at each position.

12.3.2 *Living creatures*

Neither the movements of individual limbs nor the complete locomotive process of an animate object is mechanistic. The muscles and joints of all the higher vertebrates form a highly complex system that cannot be reduced to equations in the way that a mechanism can. Moreover, man and many primates do not use this system exclusively for locomotion; they run, dance, play games, hunt, act, jump, etc. Just about the only observable constraints on such a system are the distances between the various joints. If you keep your right elbow on a horizontal surface and move your right hand to all the positions that you can, there will always be the same distance from your elbow joint to your wrist. The wrist joint moves on part of the surface of a sphere relative to the elbow. Some joints allow movement over more than a hemisphere. Other joints, such as a finger or knee, permit only circular motion of less than 180°. Hence, the starting point for computer animation of vertebrate movements is to record accurately the 3D positions of all the joints.

The process is fundamentally simple. Human performers wear dark clothing and are wired up so that there is a small spot of light at each joint. Figure 12.8 has white circles indicating some of the joints (and other salient features) that are tracked. For the best quality of animation, every joint that is used by the performer must be wired up to a real-time computer. As the person moves (against a neutral background), the electronic component at the joint samples and transmits its position in 3D to a dedicated processor. The sampling is typically at the same rate as the frames of a cinematograph film.

The computer then has a complete record of the relative movement of every joint relative to its adjacent joint. This record is then used to provide an artist with

Figure 12.8 Some of the human joints whose positions are tracked.

the kinematics of the joint, which become those of a new creature of his creation. The artist creates a new head, torso, arms, fingers, legs and feet, and clothes them however he wishes. Thus, an entirely new character is formed, and the only things that it has in common with the original are the geometry and kinematics. Of course, the new character is provided with a suitable background against which to move.

The major advantages of this technique, compared with the animation technique pioneered by Walt Disney, circa 1940, are:

- Perfect realism of movement because the motion of a living creature has been accurately recorded.

- Body contact and linking of two or more performers can be recorded accurately and transferred to the artist's creations. It is far more difficult to design even simple interactions such as hand shaking or contact dancing on a drawing board.
- The dynamics are correct and so accelerations and retardations can be shown. Early animation rarely attempted to show the start or finish of a movement, but cut from standing still to running, from running to jumping, etc. However, the original proportions and mass distribution cannot readily be modified. An animated gorilla with longer arms and broader shoulders than the performer would not appear to move naturally, because the muscular control of such a creature is significantly different.

A further advantage is that, as the record of movement is so detailed and accurate, it can be exploited for the benefit of others engaging in a similar activity. For example, teaching ballet, sports coaching, and physiotherapy. There are documented cases of field athletes whose performance has been improved following a careful analysis of and slight changes to their technique.

The process described above is only applicable to life forms that will submit to being wired up and then carry out a natural or rehearsed activity. If the creature of interest is extinct, like the dinosaur, then all that can be known about the way it moved must be derived from an analysis of its bones and joints. The makers of the programme *Walking with Dinosaurs*, first shown on BBC1 in October 1999, started from the skeletons of such reptiles. A simplified representation of the skeleton was worked out, using fossil evidence and reducing the structure to a series of balls and sticks to show axes of movement.

Palaeontology is the branch of science that deals with extinct and fossil animals and plants. From fossil evidence, experts in this field could predict the size and shape of certain dinosaurs. Guided by palaeontologists, a team of model makers produced a 'maquette' (scale model) of the extinct reptile. The maquette was laser-scanned into a computer, and hence the body of the dinosaur was computer modelled as a wire-mesh of rectangular panels, similar to that in Fig. 12.9.

At this stage, the animators had data on the body, and on the bones and joints that allowed movement of many parts of that body. They had no data on the kinematics of natural movement. If you hold a hand up in front of your eyes with the palm away from you, you can demonstrate that the movements you can make with your hand around its wrist are very similar to how you can move your head on your neck.

Glove puppeteers were coached to perform a set of choreographed movements and these were recorded in a similar manner to that described above. There are other movements that cannot be captured in that way, and it is necessary to study the locomotion of tame live animals, such as the elephant, that have similar bones and muscles. The animators make an informed guess of the motion of the extinct creature, and then go through several iterations on the computer until it looks right.

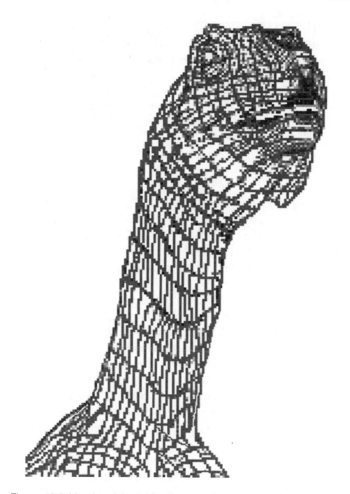

Figure 12.9 Head and neck of extinct reptile as a wire-mesh model.

12.4 **Nesting**

Nesting is the process of finding the least wasteful way of cutting several 2D shapes from a piece of stock material that is often rectangular in shape. It is a procedure that is very familiar to garment manufacturers who cut out components of a single garment from a rectangular piece of (sometimes quite expensive) material. It is also familiar to production planners who are concerned with the most efficient way of cutting sheet material into parts that will be fabricated into a complex 3D surface.

As the stock material is usually rectangular in shape, any component that is not itself rectangular will present a 'nesting' problem. Consider the nine identical

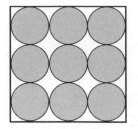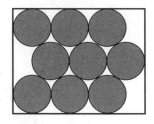

Figure 12.10 Alternative packing arrangements for nine circles.

circular parts (diameter D) shown in Fig. 12.10. In the nesting arrangement on the left, the nine circles require a rectangle of width $3D$ and height $3D$. In the nesting arrangement on the right, the same circles require a rectangle of width $3.5D$, and height $D(1 + \sqrt{3}) = 2.732D$. Apparently, the circles on the right are the more tightly packed as the space between three touching circles is smaller than the alternative arrangement.

However, the area of stock material required for the left-hand arrangement is $3D \times 3D = 9D^2$, whereas the alternative requires $3.5D \times 2.732D = 9.562D^2$. This leads to the conclusion that it is unprofitable to pack shapes closely together if this results in greater wastage around the border of the stock shape.

Of course, in practice the material may not be available in the width shown on the left of Fig. 12.10, and the nearest larger width would have to be used, thereby reducing the actual saving. The problem to be solved by nesting algorithms is not therefore simply the most efficient way of arranging the different shapes, but how to minimise the *length* of material that is required of one of the stock widths.

The optimum solution to the problem also depends upon the method that has to be employed for cutting the material. For paper, most fabrics, and thin metal sheet, the required shape is sheared out of the stock material. If the cut parts are replaced in their original positions, then there is no reduction in the total area of the material. If the manufacturing method is to use flame, laser or rotary cutting then the net area of material left after cutting is less than the gross area before cutting commenced. Moreover, the locus of the cut must not be the shape required. Instead it must be an inflation of the specified shape – see page 00.

Many nesting algorithms begin by computing the 'bounding rectangle' of all the shapes that are required in order to make one fabricated component. Consider the shapes shown in Fig. 12.11, each with its bounding rectangle. After shape E has been suitably curved, they can be bonded together to form the solid object whose front view is shown beneath its component surfaces.

It is relatively easy to design an algorithm that will butt the bounding rectangles together in a manner that reduces the waste of raw material. With the obvious exception of patterned fabrics, it generally does not matter how the shapes

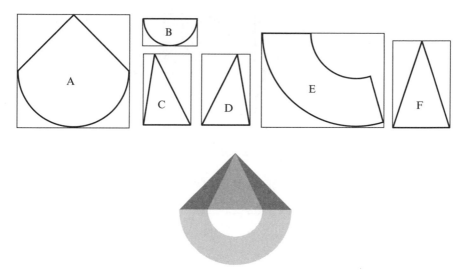

Figure 12.11 Six surfaces that form a solid object.

are oriented. Most practicable algorithms allow the user to specify the width of the stock material.

This parameter turns out to be a helpful constraint, which facilitates the design of a suitable algorithm. A relatively simple procedure can be written which tries out all the combinations of orientation and butting and discovers the minimum length of material of a specific stock width *for the bounding rectangles.*

For the six shapes shown in Fig. 12.11 we work with a two-column array in which the width of the rectangle is stored in the first column and the height in the second. Such a table is shown in Fig. 12.12.

Shape	Width mm	Height mm
A	30.0	30.0
B	15.0	7.5
C	12.5	19.1
D	12.5	19.1
E	33.1	25.4
F	15.4	23.0

Figure 12.12 Dimensions of bounding rectangles.

Generalising, if there are N shapes to be cut, then the first test is to find out if more than one rectangle can be fitted into the width, S, of the stock material. There are N ways of selecting the first shape, and 2 ways to orient it. There are $(N - 1)$ ways of selecting the second shape, and 2 ways to orient it. Hence, there

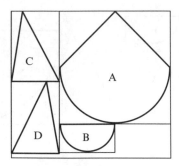

Figure 12.13 Two pairs that minimise edge wastage.

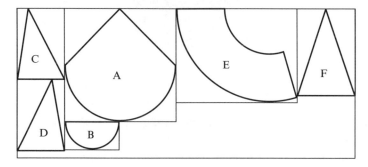

Figure 12.14 First iteration of nesting problem.

are $4N(N-1)$ combinations of two bounding rectangles, and one or more of them may be only slightly less than S. If they all exceed S then there is no alternative but to cut only one shape from the width of the material.

Suppose that we specify a stock material of width 40 mm, and look at all the ways of combining two rectangles, using the dimensions in Fig. 12.12. A simple procedure can discover that the closest to stock width is achieved by adding the height of C to the height of D, to give 38.2 mm. As the *widths* of C and D are the same, this would be an advantageous combination with which to begin. The procedure will also show that the height of A added to the height of B gives 37.5 mm, and so that combination could be placed alongside C and D to give the arrangement shown in Fig. 12.13.

The remaining rectangles, E and F, cannot be butted together so as to take up less than 40 mm. They have to be placed next to A and B and oriented so as to take up the shortest possible length of stock material. This is shown in Fig. 12.14, which clearly indicates the complexity of automating nesting operations.

The reader's eye–brain system can probably find a less wasteful way of arranging these six shapes on the stock material.

Figure 12.14 may be regarded as the first iteration towards an optimal solution to the problem of cutting shapes A–F from material that is 40.0 mm wide.

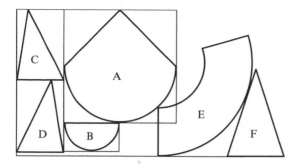

Figure 12.15 Better packing after transformation and collision detection.

Clearly, this is nowhere near the goal, but equally it is far from being the worst case scenario of maximum wastage.

Full details of commercial nesting algorithms are rarely published, as they are valuable intellectual property. Nevertheless, observation of nesting algorithms in operation suggests that one optimisation technique is to investigate if it is possible to rotate and/or translate any of the abutting rectangles so that they overlap without their corresponding shapes overlapping. For example, in Fig. 12.14, shape E could be rotated through 90° anticlockwise and moved downwards and to its left before it intersects shape A. Shape F can then be translated until one of its sides is tangential to an arc on Shape E. The new arrangement is illustrated in Fig. 12.15. The operation of checking how close one shape can approach another is often called 'collision detection'. It is a complex process, especially when higher-order (e.g. Bézier) curves are present.

More sophisticated nesting procedures rotate the shapes until they are 'well packed' into their bounding rectangles. The theory being that, if as little material as possible is wasted inside each rectangle, then the first iteration solution will be better than that illustrated in Fig. 12.14. If collision detection is applied to the well-packed shapes, then it may be possible to save even more material.

Nesting algorithms present such a fascinating intellectual challenge that it is easy to overlook the economics. The costs of developing software are always recovered either by selling a licence to users, or by providing a bureau service. If the stock material is very expensive and/or the product is to be manufactured in very large numbers, then the cost of purchasing a computer solution should be recoverable by savings in material quantity, transport costs, and reduction of inventory.

12.5 Image enhancement

Colour images become available either by digital photography or by digital scanning. Undoubtedly, digital photography will replace film in the very near future as cameras giving 2048 × 1536 pixels become affordable. This resolution is the maximum that the human eye can resolve on 35 mm film. There are many reasons why it is desirable to carry out some processing of the image, and some frequently used techniques are listed below.

- *Image redesign.* A large class of applications of particular interest to commercial artists and advertisers involves geometric transformations of images and applications of visual effects. This class includes animations, dissolves, mosaics, and fractal transformations.
- *Noise removal.* The transmission of graphical images, particularly from low-power transmitters in space, can result in loss of information and the introduction of noise in various forms. Image processing techniques such as smoothing can help to suppress image noise, but at the expense of some blurring of edges and fine detail in the image.
- *Distortion removal.* Image acquisition techniques can introduce distortion into the original image. If the form of the distortion is known (e.g. by photographing a square grid), it is a relatively simple task to recover an undistorted image by mapping out the distortion.
- *Blur removal.* Photographs of moving objects often entail objectionable blurring which the appropriate image transformation process readily removes.
- *Image enhancement.* The quality of images can usually be improved by adjusting the brightness and contrast parameters. In addition to the intensity contrast, image-processing techniques are available for improving the geometric contrast of objects by edge enhancements.
- *Computer vision.* The objective of computer vision is to understand the contents of an image. This involves complex pattern recognition processes that usually begin with edge detection and object segmentation. A number of image processing functions are available to carry out these tasks.
- *Visualization.* Numerous image-processing functions are available for transforming images into alternative representations to assist the user in understanding and extracting meaning from the image. These include colour mapping, contour mapping, 3D histogramming of 2D intensity data, and slicing of 3D images.

12.5.1 *RGB colour model*

Based upon the 'tristimulus' theory of vision, human eyes perceive colour through the stimulation of three visual pigments in the cones of the retina. These visual pigments have a peak sensitivity at wavelengths of about 630 nm (red), 530 nm (green), and 450 nm (blue). By comparing intensities in a light source, we perceive the colour of the light. This theory of vision is the basis for displaying colour output on a video monitor using the three colour primaries, red, green and blue, referred to as the RGB colour model.

We can represent this model with a unit cube defined on R, G, and B axes, as shown in Fig. 12.16. The origin represents black, and the vertex with coordinates

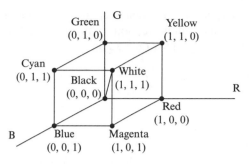

Figure 12.16 The RGB colour model.

(1, 1, 1) is white. Vertices of the cube on the axes represent the primary colours, and the remaining vertices represent the complementary colour for each of the primary colours.

Notice that the line joining Black to White in Fig. 12.16 represents a grey-scale. The RGB colour scheme is an additive model. Intensities of the primary colours are added to produce other colours. Each colour point within the bounds of the cube can be represented as the triple (R, G, B), where values for R, G, and B are assigned in the range from 0 to 1. Thus a colour C_λ is expressed in RGB components as

$$C_\lambda = R\mathbf{R} + G\mathbf{G} + B\mathbf{B}$$

For example, the yellow vertex is obtained by adding red and green to produce the triple (1, 1, 0). Shades of grey are represented along the main diagonal of the cube from black at the origin to the white vertex. Each point along this greyscale diagonal has an equal contribution from each primary colour.

12.5.2 *The Laplacian operator*

Several standard mathematical operations are useful in transforming graphical images. The image is defined as an intensity function:

$f(x, y)$, at pixel location (x, y).

For grey scale images, $f(x, y)$ may be represented by an 8-bit value in which 0 corresponds to black and 255 corresponds to white. For 8-bit colour, $f(x, y)$ represents 256 addresses to a colour look-up table representing the colour palette. For 24-bit colour, $f(x, y)$ corresponds to a 24-bit code in which the red, blue, and green intensities are each encoded with 8-bit segments. Such encoding is equivalent to three overlapping 8-bit intensity functions:

$f_R(x, y), f_G(x, y)$ and $f_B(x, y)$.

Edge detection is typically the first step in the image segmentation, pre-processing phase of object identification. The most useful function for edge detection is the Laplacian operator defined as

$$\nabla^2 f(x, y) = \frac{\partial^2 f(x, y)}{\partial x^2} + \frac{\partial^2 f(x, y)}{\partial y^2}$$

Readers who are not familiar with partial differentiation may find it helpful to have the above terms expressed in words. $\partial f / \partial x$ is the rate at which f changes with respect to x while y remains constant. $\partial f / \partial y$ is the rate at which f changes with respect to y while x remains constant. $\partial^2 f / \partial x^2$ is the rate at which $\partial f / \partial x$ changes with respect to x while y remain constant. $\partial^2 f / \partial y^2$ is the rate at which $\partial f / \partial y$ changes with respect to y while x remains constant.

Consider changes with respect to x: immediately before (x, y) the value of the function changes from $f(x - 1, y)$ to $f(x, y)$. Hence, on one side of this position $\partial f / \partial x = f(x, y) - f(x - 1, y)$. Similarly, just after (x, y), $\partial f / \partial x = f(x + 1, y) - f(x, y)$. Hence, the rate of change of $\partial f / \partial x$ with respect to x is:

$$f(x + 1, y) - f(x, y) - (f(x, y) - f(x - 1, y)) = f(x + 1, y) + f(x - 1, y) - 2f(x, y)$$

Similarly, the rate of change of $\partial f / \partial y$ with respect to y is:

$$f(x, y + 1) + f(x, y - 1) - 2f(x, y)$$

Hence, the five-point Laplacian computed by taking differences from the four nearest neighbour pixels and assuming $Dx = Dy = 1$ is

$$\nabla^2 f(x, y) = f(x + 1, y) + f(x - 1, y) + f(x, y + 1) + f(x, y - 1) - 4f(x, y)$$

The five-point Laplacian is computed by taking -4 times the value of the current pixel and adding to this value the value of the pixel immediately above, below, to the right, and to the left of it. This can be summarised as applying the following 3×3 window to each pixel:

$$\begin{vmatrix} 0 & 1 & 0 \\ 1 & -4 & 1 \\ 0 & 1 & 0 \end{vmatrix}$$ the matrix form of the five-point Laplacian operator.

The effect of this Laplacian operator can be readily demonstrated even when the greyscale only has a range of 0.7. Figure 12.17 shows a 16×16 array of digits with a large block of 7's near the centre. These pixel values have been mapped on the right of the figure.

When the Laplacian is applied to the central 14×14 array shown in Fig. 12.17, the resulting matrix is as shown in Fig. 12.18.

```
0 0 1 1 2 2 0 0 2 2 1 1 0 0 0 0
0 0 1 1 2 1 0 0 2 2 1 1 0 0 0 0
0 0 1 1 1 7 7 7 7 7 1 1 0 0 0 0
0 0 1 1 7 7 7 7 7 7 1 0 0 0 0 0
0 0 1 7 7 7 7 7 7 7 7 0 0 0 0 0
0 0 7 7 7 7 7 7 7 7 7 7 0 0 0 0
0 7 7 7 7 7 7 7 7 7 7 7 7 0 0 0
0 7 7 7 7 7 7 7 7 7 7 7 7 0 0 0
0 7 7 7 7 7 7 7 7 7 7 7 7 0 0 0
0 7 7 7 7 7 3 3 3 3 7 7 7 7 0 0
0 0 7 7 7 7 3 3 3 3 7 7 7 7 0 0
0 0 7 7 7 7 3 3 3 3 7 7 7 7 0 0
0 0 7 7 7 7 3 3 3 3 7 7 7 7 0 0
0 0 1 7 7 7 3 3 3 3 7 7 7 0 0 0
0 0 1 1 2 2 0 0 2 1 1 1 0 0 0 0
0 0 1 1 2 2 0 0 2 2 1 1 0 0 0 0
```

Figure 12.17 Black shape with edge to be detected.

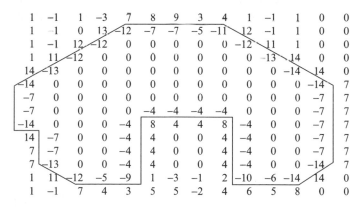

Figure 12.18 Laplacian applied to Fig. 12.17.

Notice the large number of zero values, which occur because:

$$f(x + 1, y) + f(x - 1, y) + f(x, y + 1) + f(x, y - 1) - 4f(x, y) = 0$$

In other words, the pixel at (x, y) is surrounded by four pixels of the same greyscale value as itself. An edge can be detected by tracing the path along which output from the Laplacian changes sign. One such path has been traced on Fig. 12.18, and it is identical to the shape in the central area of Fig. 12.17.

Edge detection can be exploited to emphasise what would otherwise be subtle differences when the image is viewed. A plot of sea temperature, for example, can be made clearer if there is greater differentiation between the blocks of colour that make up the image. Fig 12.19 has been produced by suitable changes to the greyscale of each block of colour in Fig. 12.17.

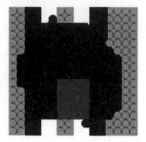

Figure 12.19 Increased contrast between blocks of colour.

12.5.3 *Image sharpening*

One source of image blurring in photography is the diffusion of dyes across sharp boundaries of the image. The time-dependent diffusion equation is given by

$$\frac{\partial g}{\partial t} = k\nabla^2 g$$

where

$g(x, y, t)$ is the time-dependent degraded image, and

$g(x, y, 0) = f(x, y)$ is the original, unblurred image.

By expanding $g(x, y, t)$ around the latter time, $t = \tau$, and keeping only the first-order term, the original image, $f(x, y)$, can be restored by

$$f(x, y) = g(x, y, t) - \tau k\nabla^2 g$$

The time taken to effect the degree of blurring evident in the image is irrelevant, and so we can set $\tau k = 1$ for algebraic convenience. We then have:

$$f(x, y) = g(x, y) - \nabla^2 g$$

or

$$f(x, y) = g(x, y)$$
$$- (g(x+1, y) + g(x-1, y) + g(x, y+1) + g(x, y-1) - 4g(x, y))$$
$$= 5g(x, y) - g(x+1, y) - g(x-1, y) - g(x, y+1) - g(x, y-1)$$

This is another useful application of the Laplacian operator and may be represented in terms of discrete pixel coordinates by the five-point window operator:

$$\begin{bmatrix} 0 & -1 & 0 \\ -1 & 5 & -1 \\ 0 & -1 & 0 \end{bmatrix}$$ matrix form of the five-point restoration operator

12.6 Charting

Arguably, one of the most difficult charts to generate by computer is a diagram of individuals descended from a common ancestor – a 'Descendancy Chart'. The converse chart (often called a 'Pedigree Chart') is simple by comparison, because every individual has two parents, four grandparents, eight great-grandparents, etc. Figure 12.20 is a typical pedigree chart. The algorithm that draws it has to make no decisions about spacing. It simply reads data recorded about an individual and puts it into the right box.

Notice that only the following graphics constructs are used:

- horizontal and vertical lines,
- rectangles,
- text.

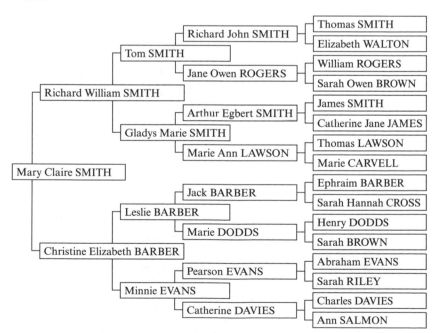

Figure 12.20 A pedigree chart showing five generations.

Most charts use only a small subset of the available graphics routines. The principal difficulty in drawing charts is not the output of entities themselves, but the positioning relative to each other. In the case of a pedigree chart, selection of the appropriate position for a particular box is facilitated by a convention that the father of individual no. I is no. $2I$ and the mother is no. $2I + 1$. Hence, if the subject is No. 1 then their father's details go into box No. 2, and their mother's details into box No. 3. Father's father (paternal grandfather) fits into box $2 \times 2 = 4$ and the paternal grandmother goes into $4 + 1 = 5$, etc.

Contrast this simplicity with a descendancy chart. In any particular generation, there can be any number of direct descendants, and it is normal to show the spouses of these descendants, especially if they became parents and contributed their genes to the descendants of the subject. An additional complication is that the subject of the chart and any number of descendants may have had more than one spouse, and had children with each of them. King Henry VIII had children by three of his six wives. He married Catherine of Aragon in 1509 and Princess Mary (Mary I) was born in 1516. He then married Anne Boleyn in 1533, the same year that Princess Elizabeth (Elizabeth I) was born. Anne was beheaded and Henry married Jane Seymour in 1536. Henry's desperately sought son Edward VI was born in 1537. These three children, the only descendants of Henry VIII, are shown in Fig. 12.21.

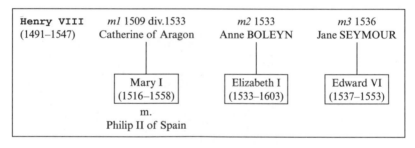

Figure 12.21 Descendants of King Henry VIII of England.

Fortunately for automatic chart generation, none of Henry's children had offspring, but family history is not always so conveniently simple. When designing chart-drawing algorithms, a thorough knowledge of the domain to which they relate is essential. Henry VIII was chosen because his well-known six marriages causes considerable spatial planning problems.

However, knowledge of genealogy tends to the conclusion that three marriages *with children* will be a great rarity. Hence, software can be designed to cope with up to two marriages having issue, plus perhaps one or two childless marriages.

The need for some system of record structuring is evident. Obviously, there will have to be two types of record:

- individual records,
- family records.

An individual record must have a pointer to the family headed by the individual's mother and father. A family record must have pointers to the individual record of the husband and wife.

For a pedigree chart, records with the above links will suffice, as all that is required is to link from an individual to his/her parents. Hence there would be a link from Elizabeth I to a family headed by Henry VIII and Ann Boleyn. This data structure could be used when drawing a descendancy chart, but a great deal of searching is required. To find all the children of Henry VIII, it would be necessary first to inspect all the family records and filter those where Henry VIII is the husband. Then the individual records are inspected looking for people whose parents' marriage is one of the marriages of Henry VIII.

The general point to be made here is that, although the above record structure is a *true* model of sexual (male/female) reproduction, it is far from being a *convenient* model because of the significant amount of searching that has to be done. This is a situation that arises in many computer applications, and the cure is either to add redundant data to the structure, or to pre-process the minimal model so that searching is eliminated.

A practicable structure can be specified by adding some redundancies both to the individual and to the family record. By definition, redundant data are not essential, but highly desirable because of the time saved. Thus, an individual record will have details of all the families where the subject is a spouse, and there would be six links from the individual record of Henry VIII. Similarly, there would be a link from the family headed by Henry and Catherine of Aragon to the child Mary, etc.

This makes the task far simpler. To find all the children of Henry, the algorithm works through all six of his recorded marriages and looks up the children of each union. As none of these children had children themselves, the Tudor dynasty came to an end with the death of Elizabeth I in 1603, so we need an example of complex descendancy in order to examine the process of chart generation.

Figure 12.22 shows how both the naturalist Charles Darwin and his wife Emma (née Wedgwood) were descended from Josiah Wedgwood. Josiah was the maternal grandfather of Charles, and he was the paternal grandfather of Emma. Hence, Charles and Emma were first cousins and so they each appear twice in Fig. 12.22, once as a direct descendant, and once as the spouse of a direct descendant. Using recursion, the type of chart exemplified by Fig. 12.22 is easily generated from lineage-linked data. The algorithm merely has to insert a vertical line beneath a marriage and short horizontal lines for each child of a marriage. The vertical line is moved right a fixed distance for each successive generation.

There are several commercial programs that will automatically generate a reasonable-looking descendancy chart. The authors of such software have

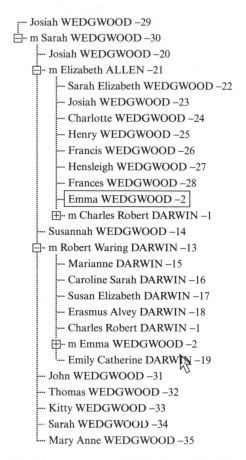

Figure 12.22 Descent from Josiah Wedgwood (1730–1795).

usually tried to take into account the following conventions that are widely accepted by genealogists and family historians. Inevitably, it is impracticable to adhere to all such conventions.

- The husband's name is on the left, the wife's on the right, linked by *m* for married. An = sign is often used instead, but this leaves the problem of how to express other unions that produce children.
- From the marriage symbol comes a line of descent, which spreads out horizontally to accommodate the names of all the children, ideally set out equally on each side of the *m* symbol. As far as possible, the descent line to each child should be central to its name.
- The names of the children appear in birth order.
- A twice-married man is flanked by his two wives, in order, and the descent line runs from each marriage symbol to their own group of children.

- If there are three marriages with children, then the second wife appears centrally, under the name of her husband, which still allows the children to be set out in chronological order.
- The names of children in the same generation should ideally be entered in the same horizontal line in chronological order.
- When a marriage between first cousins unites the children of non-consecutive siblings, a clearer chart can be drawn by placing a child next to its spouse/cousin. The disadvantage of this arrangement is that one set of children will not be shown in birth order.
- Second or third cousin marriages and inter-generation marriages (e.g. cousins once removed) create similar spatial problems. Annotation is the only practicable solution.
- Illegitimate children are shown with a line of descent from both parents, if known, or from the mother alone. The child can be shown with a dashed line and the surname by which it is commonly known.
- Twins are shown by branching a single descent line.

In order to generate a descendancy chart, it is essential first to compute its overall dimensions. The vertical distance is obvious – it is simply the number of generations (including the ancestor) that the user wishes to have charted. Less obvious is the fact that the maximum horizontal distance is that required for the generation that has the largest total of descendants plus their spouses. To find the generation with the greatest number of direct descendants plus their spouses, the following variables are required.

Ancestor	*Reference No. of common ancestor*
CurrentGeneration	*Starts at 1 for common ancestor*
BiggestGeneration	*No. of generation with most people*
HowBig	*Total number in BiggestGeneration*
TotalDescendants	*Total in current generation*
GrandTotal	*Total of Descendants plus Spouses*
ThisGeneration	*Array of Personal Reference Numbers*
NextGeneration	*Array of Personal Reference Numbers*
TotalInNextGeneration	*Total in next generation*
PersonCount	*Index of current person*
Subject	*Personal Reference No.*
NumberOfMarriages	*Total of recorded marriages of Subject*
MarriageCount	*Index of current marriage*
NumberOfChildren	*Total for current marriage*

The algorithm could be outlined like this.

1. Set CurrentGeneration = 0. Set BiggestGeneration = 1. Set HowBig = 1.
2. Increment CurrentGeneration. Set TotalDescendants = 1. Set ThisGeneration[1] = Ancestor.
3. Set NextGeneration to EMPTY. Set TotalInNextGeneration = 0.

4. Set PersonCount = 1. Set GrandTotal = TotalPersons.
5. Set Subject = ThisGeneration[PersonCount].
   Look up NumberOfMarriages of Subject.
   If there are no marriages then go to step 9.
6. Set MarriageCount = 1.
7. Increment GrandTotal.
   Look up NumberOfChildren of current marriage and add each of them to
   NextGeneration, incrementing TotalInNextGeneration.
8. Increment MarriageCount. If MarriageCount ≤ NumberOfMarriages then
   go to step 7.
9. Increment PersonCount. If PersonCount ≤ TotalDescendants then go to step 5.
10. If GrandTotal > HowBig then set HowBig = GrandTotal *and* set
    BiggestGeneration = CurrentGeneration. Set ThisGeneration =
    NextGeneration. Set TotalPersons = TotalInNextGeneration.
    If TotalDescendants > 0 *and* ThisGeneration is not the last to be charted
    then go to step 2.

The above algorithm would discover that

BiggestGeneration = 3 and
HowBig = 16   for the data shown in Fig. 12.22.

For clarity, Fig. 12.23 only shows one line of descent – that from Josiah Wedgwood to one of his distinguished great-grandsons, George Howard Darwin, FRS.

Notice how the genealogical program has indicated the two appearances of the parents of George: Emma Wedgwood is labelled [1] and Charles Darwin is labelled [2] to emphasise that they are the same individuals. The program has been instructed not to repeat the descendants of individuals who appear twice

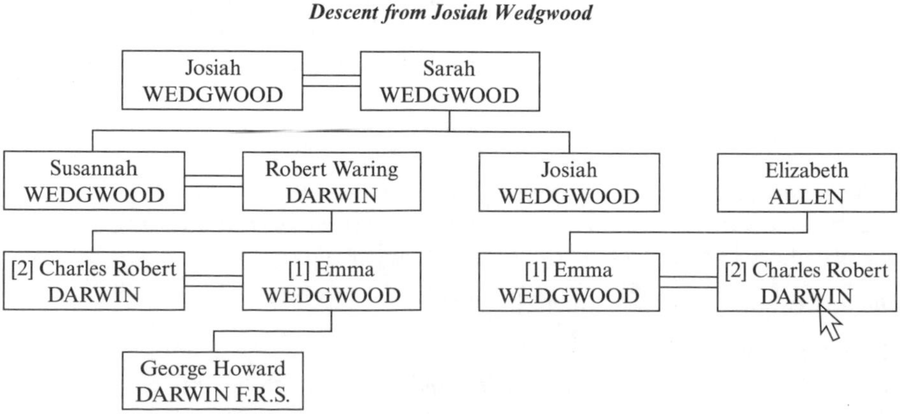

Descent from Josiah Wedgwood

Figure 12.23 Offspring from marriage of first cousins shown only once.

Descent from Josiah Wedgwood

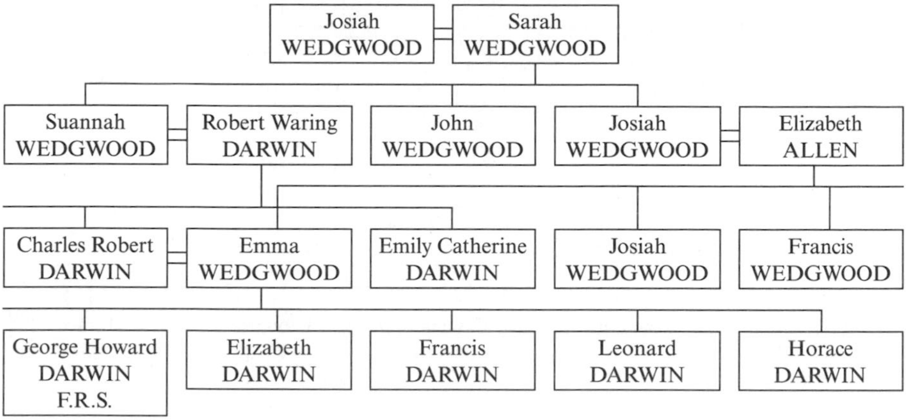

Figure 12.24 Siblings of married cousins included.

in the chart, otherwise there would be another descent line from the box indicated with an arrow.

Although few commercial programs have this facility, it is not difficult to write a procedure that eliminates the duplication altogether, by staggering the horizontal link lines in order to indicate the parents of both spouses who are first cousins. The staggering is essential if siblings of the cousins who married are to be shown. The chart would then be arranged as in Fig. 12.24. The revised chart is reasonably clear, although a pedant might protest that the children of Josiah Wedgwood and Elizabeth Allen are no longer in birth order.

Notice how, in Fig. 12.23 and Fig. 12.24, there is an = sign to indicate a union and any children of that union are connected to the *spouse* of the direct descendant. This solves the problem posed by two marriages, as one spouse can appear on the left and the other on the right of the direct descendant. This convention has to be slightly modified for implementation in a genealogical program: the = signs may need to be stretched because of space requirements below them. This type of implementation is illustrated in Fig. 12.25.

The generation with the largest number of members is drawn first, starting with the visible rectangles containing personal details. A vertical line is drawn upwards from the centre of each rectangle to the parent/child interface. If the number of children is greater than one, then a spanning line is put in from the first to the last child and then a vertical line is drawn upwards from the midpoint of the child-spanning line to end half way up the vertical interface between the parents.

Note also that it is the *children* of this largest generation who determine the horizontal position of the *parents*, and not vice versa. Individuals in this generation may themselves be parents and so the position of their children is fixed by

Descendants from Erasmus Darwin

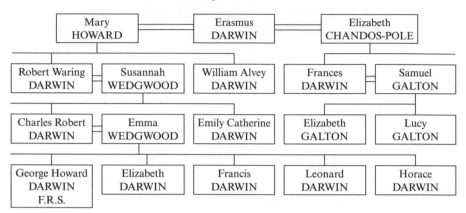

Figure 12.25 Descent from two marriages.

the parents. By definition, there cannot be a *larger* number of individuals in the generation immediately after that with the *largest*, but there could be an equal number.

Hence, the algorithm cannot be allowed to arrange children symmetrically beneath their parents. Instead, the children and their spouses are first positioned by single cell increments for each individual. When that has been done, any cells unoccupied on the right are used to move children more nearly beneath their parents. A useful constraint is that some point on the child-spanning line must be vertically beneath the spouse who sired or bore these children.

It is stated above that some abstract concepts are hard to fathom unless they are presented graphically. We have now examined one such concept, and seen how conventions that were developed for hand-drawn charts have to be adapted and modified so that clear, useful charts can be computer generated.

12.7 **Summary**

- *Morphing* is the transformation of object shapes from one form to another. The process is carried out one key-frame at a time, and the number of lines in a key-frame generally changes from one to the next. The fundamental problem is therefore that of equalising the number of lines in consecutive frames. This can sometimes be done automatically, but more often the process requires interaction with a creative software user.
- *Animation* is the process of showing accurate or realistic movement on a VDU. By definition, the positions of all the components of a mechanism are computable when the position of any one component has been specified. Hence, a mechanism can be animated once its geometry has

been analysed – the solution is entirely mathematical. By contrast, the motion of a living creature has to treated empirically. The positions of a large number of the creature's joints are sampled at suitable intervals. These data can be analysed for studies of locomotion, sporting perform- ance, etc. They can also be used as the kinematics of a fictitious life-form (with a very similar anatomy) created by an artist. Based upon advice from palaeontologists, it is possible to create solid scale models of extinct life-forms. Some joint movements may be animated by recording glove puppet performances.

- *Nesting* is the process of finding the least wasteful way of cutting several 2D shapes from a piece of stock material that is often rectangular in shape. Apart from the 'bounding rectangle' technique and general papers on 'collision detection', almost nothing has been published about nesting algorithms. With contemporary very-high-speed processors, it possible to use 'trial and error' paradigms that use up considerable CPU time, but are able to discover optimal solutions more quickly and cheaply than a person can by shuffling paper templates around.
- *Image enhancement* has many applications. These range from the cos- metic, such as bringing out more detail from a scanned photograph, to the life saving, such as advance warning of natural disasters. The image is defined as an intensity function $f(x, y)$, at pixel location (x, y). If the image is time dependent, then the function is written $g(x, y, t)$. Either type of function may be digitally processed in order to yield some specific, beneficial result.
- *Charting* has been defined as the automatic generation of a diagram that renders some abstract concept clearer and more meaningful to the viewer. Some concepts, such as annual expenditure, birth and death rates, and election results have no established conventions about how data should be presented. Others, such as physical and political boundaries, genealogy, and project planning do have some accepted conventions. Such conventions may be taken into account by software writers, but it is rarely practicable to conform slavishly to them, and adaptation is required.

12.8 **Further reading**

McLaughlin, E., *Laying out a Pedigree*, Federation of Family History Societies, 1988. Intended for Family Historians. A well-illustrated survey of custom and practice in the genealogical profession.

Griffiths, G., *The Essence of Structured Systems Analysis Techniques*, Prentice Hall Europe, 1998. Contains lots of Entity Relationship diagrams for exer- cise 6 below.

Cawsey, A., *The Essence of Artificial Intelligence*, Prentice Hall Europe, 1998. Deals with edge detection applied to robot vision.

Glossary Working Party (Editor), *A Glossary of Computing Terms*, Longman Group Limited, 1995. Generally useful, and also has examples of system flowcharts for exercise 6 below.

O'Rourke, M., *Principles of Three-Dimensional Computer Animation*, W. W. Norton & Company, 1998. Many of the techniques that were experimental when this book was written have since become an accepted part of computer animation technology.

Exercises

1. Use tracing paper to reproduce the mask of comedy and the mask of tragedy shown below. Use a ruler so that each mask is comprised entirely of short straight lines.

    Count the number of lines in each mask and determine the number that need to be added or subtracted in order to morph one mask into the other. If you have the facilities available, you could digitise each mask into a computer system and write a program to carry out the morphing process.

2. The mechanism shown below is a '4-bar chain'.

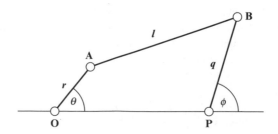

Link 0A (radius r) rotates continuously and the connecting link AB (length l) will cause link BP (radius q) to oscillate.

In order to animate this mechanism, it is necessary to know the relationship between angle θ and angle ϕ. There is tutorial material at these web sites

www.cs.cmu.edu/People/rapidproto/mechanisms/chapt5.html
web.usna.navy.mil/~mecheng/DESIGN/CAD/

Write a program that will display the three moving links in their correct positions at a suitable increment of θ.

3. Trace the six shapes shown in Fig. 12.11 on to card and cut them out. By shuffling these templates around, find the shortest length of stock material of the width shown in Fig. 12.13. Have any of the shapes been rotated through an angle that is not a multiple of 90°? If you were writing a nesting program, would you abandon the 'bounding rectangle' technique? If so, what would you replace it by?

4. Write a program to detect any edges that are present in the 0–7 greyscale image shown below.

```
2  1  2  5  5  5  5  3  3  3  3  3  0  0  0  0
1  2  1  5  5  5  3  3  3  3  3  3  3  0  0  0
2  1  2  5  5  3  2  3  2  3  2  3  2  3  0  0
1  2  1  5  3  2  3  3  2  3  2  3  2  3  0  0
2  1  2  5  3  3  2  3  2  3  2  3  2  3  0  0
1  2  1  5  3  2  5  3  3  2  3  3  7  6  6  7
2  1  2  5  3  2  5  3  3  3  3  3  6  7  7  6
1  2  1  5  3  2  5  3  2  3  3  3  7  7  6  6
2  1  2  5  3  3  5  3  3  2  3  3  6  6  7  7
1  2  1  5  3  3  5  3  3  3  3  2  3  6  6  6
2  1  2  5  3  3  5  3  2  2  3  3  2  7  7  7
1  2  1  5  5  5  5  3  2  3  2  3  3  6  7  6
2  1  2  5  5  5  5  3  2  3  3  3  3  7  7  6
2  1  2  5  5  5  5  2  3  3  3  3  2  6  6  7
2  2  2  5  5  5  5  2  3  2  3  3  1  5  5  6
2  2  2  5  5  5  5  3  3  3  3  3  1  4  5  5
```

5. Study the conventions (or standards) that are adopted for one of the following types of chart:

(a) entity relationship diagram, as used in systems analysis,
(b) a system flowchart,
(c) a dimensioned engineering drawing.

Suggest a suitable data structure for recording the features that are found in the chart. Discuss how many of the conventions could actually be adopted if the chart were computer-generated.

Index

2D Shapes
  boolean operations, 38, 47, 97, 100
  deflation, 41
  disjointedness, 26, 27
  inflation, 34, 40, 41, 42, 43, 44, 47

Algorithm
  inflation/deflation, 40, 41, 42, 43, 44
  inside/outside test, 34, 35, 36, 37, 38
American National Standards Institute
  (ANSI), 4
Angle
  rotation, 30, 31, 67
Animation, 168–173
  Living creatures, 170–172
  Mechanisms, 168–170
Axis
  rotation, 30, 31, 67

B-Rep, 95, 101, 110, 112, 122
Bézier
  curves, 26, 51–55, 59
  parametric cubic, 51
  surface, 56–60
Boolean algebra
  AND, 39
  difference, 39, 40, 100, 101
  inclusive OR, 38
  intersection, 39, 99
  union, 38, 39, 101
Boundary fill algorithms
  4-connected region, 135, 136
  8-connected region, 136
Boundary representation, 95, 101, 115, 116,
  122
Bounding
  rectangle, 174, 175
Braid, 5, 7, 111
Bresenham's algorithm, 5, 7, 14, 129–135,
  139
Brownian motion, 82

Cathode ray tube (CRT), 1, 2, 6
Chart
  descendency, 183, 184, 185, 187
  pedigree, 183, 185
Charting, 163, 183–190, 191
Circle drawing algorithm
  Bresenham, 133–135
Clipping, 4, 7
Colour model
  RGB, 178–179
Computer-aided design, 3, 46, 57
Computer-aided manufacture, 3, 34
Constant-intensity shading, 150, 160
Constructive Solid Geometry (CSG), 7, 47,
  99–102, 110, 127
  primitives, 5, 99–101, 110
Coordinates
  Cartesian, 9–14, 17, 20, 25, 62,
  homogeneous, 18–22, 62–65, 73
  polar, 12–14, 83
Curved surface
  quadric, 127
  superquadric, 104, 156
Curves
  approximate operation, 49
  control points, 51–58
  interpolate operation, 49–50

Direct-view storage tube, 2, 3,
  Tektronix, 2

Fractals
  deterministic, 77, 79
  generator, 77
  initiator, 77
  invariant set, 80
  Julia set, 83–89
  Koch curve, 77, 79
  Mandelbrot set, 83, 89–92
  modelling plants, 80
  self-affine, 80, 82

self-similar, 77, 80, 81
self-squaring, 80, 83–91
stochastic, 79, 80

Geometric models, 34, 94, 111
Geometric properties, 34, 44–46, 97, 116
Geometry
  circular arc, 14–17, 42
  radius of curvature, 50, 59
Gouraud shading, 59, 151–153, 161
Graph theory
  circuit, 25, 27, 28, 35, 37, 39, 40, 44, 45,
    95, 98, 123, 125
  closed path, 25
  connectivity, 25
  degree of a node, 25
  di-edge, 25
  digraph, 25, 34, 38, 41, 44
  edge, 25, 95, 96, 97, 98
  edge-sequence, 25
  length of edge-sequence, 25
  loop, 25
  nodes, 25–27, 29, 33, 101, 106–110, 146
  node-set, 25
  path, 25
  simple graph, 25, 33
  trail, 25
Graphics Kernel System (GKS), 4, 6–8

Illumination model
  ambient light, 147, 159
  diffuse reflection, 147, 148
  Lambertian reflector, 147
  reflections 159
  shadows, 158, 159
Image enhancement, 177, 178
Image processing, 177, 178
International Standards Organisation
    (ISO), 4, 7

Koch curve, 77, 79

Lambertian reflector, 147
Laplacian, 179–181, 183
Light
  ambient, 147, 159
  diffuse reflection, 147, 148
Line
  clipping, 4, 7
  parametric form, 21–22
Line drawing algorithm
  Bresenham, 5, 7, 8

Mach band, 153, 160
Mandelbrot set, 83, 89–92
Matrix
  column vector, 18, 62
  multiplication, 31
  row vector, 20, 62
Modelling
  packages, 6, 99–101
  primitives, 5, 99–101, 110
Morphing, 164–168, 190
  key frame, 164–167

Nesting, 173–177, 191
Newell
  equations, 69–70, 73

Octree encoding, 105, 107, 110, 111

Painter's algorithm, 118–120, 126
Parameters, 17, 21, 50, 56, 57
Phong shading, 59, 153–154, 160
Pixel, 2, 106–108, 110, 122, 124, 126, 127,
    129–137, 144–146, 153–155

Quadtree encoding, 105–110

Raster graphics, 2–3, 129
  bitmap, 34
Ray casting, 143–144
  visible surface, 144
Ray tracing, 144–149
  basic algorithm, 145
Rotation
  matrix representation, 32
  three-dimensional, 67–69
  two-dimensional, 30–32

Scaling
  factors, 30
  matrix representation, 31
  three-dimensional, 66–67
  two-dimensional, 30–31
Shadows
  computation, 158–159
Sketchpad, 3, 6, 7,
Sutherland, 3, 6, 7, 127

Texture, 154–159, 161
Transformations
  matrix, 31–32, 66–68
  rotation, 30–32, 67–69
  scaling, 30–31, 66–67
  translation, 29, 31, 66

Viewport, 4, 9, 10, 79, 87, 90, 142
Visible surface problem
   Painter's algorithm, 118–120, 126
   Scan line algorithm, 72, 122–126
   Warnockís algorithm, 120–122,
     127

Visual Man
   Web site, 26

Web sites, 26, 165, 193
Window, 4, 76, 90, 180, 183
Windows (Microsoft), 135